CREATING · STYLE · WITH ·

HOUSEPLANTS

CREATING · STYLE · WITH ·

HOUSEPLANTS

JANE NEWDICK
DAVID SQUIRE

GALLERY BOOKS
An Imprint of W. H. Smith Publishers Inc.
112 Madison Avenue
New York City 10016

First published 1985 by
Octopus Books Limited
59 Grosvenor Street
London W1

This edition published 1986 by Gallery Books
An imprint of W.H. Smith Publishers Inc.
112 Madison Avenue, New York, N.Y. 10016

ISBN 0 8317 1856 0

Printed in Hong Kong

CONTENTS

INTRODUCTION

I have lived in the country for most of my life and am surrounded by plants both wild and cultivated, but even with such a profusion outside I could not live in a house which didn't have some green or flowering plants in most rooms. At the last count I had 28 different varieties but there have been times when I have had many more. A house with no flowers or plants in it feels strange to me. It may be beautifully designed, wonderfully furnished and immaculately looked after but if it has no plants, it will feel cold, unloved and quite simply not alive.

City and country dwellers derive equal pleasure from houseplants, I'm sure, especially in our unpredictable climate with its brief summers where greenness has an especially therapeutic value. The sales of indoor plants keep climbing year by year as more and more people discover the pleasures of indoor gardening.

There are plenty of books that deal with this aspect of the subject but *Creating Style with Houseplants* aims to do something quite different and new. This book shows how to bring houseplants into an overall decorative scheme and use them in a way that is both sympathetic to their form and shape and also to their horticultural needs.

Many plants are bought with a particular position in mind but very often, and I'm definitely guilty of this, a plant is purely an impulse buy, something you can't resist and is bought with little thought of where to put it. Well, this book can help both those who regularly find themselves outside a shop with an armful of pots containing plants they hadn't intended to buy as well as those more restrained plant purchasers who buy for a specific purpose. This book will make you look at your house, room by room, in a new way and hopefully you'll discover dozens of novel places where you can put all the plants you'd like to own as well as how to make the best of those you've already got.

Jane Newdick

HOME SETTING

Houseplants can be used in a wide variety of ways to add atmosphere to your home and to give your decoration character and individuality. The choice of plants available is extensive and by careful selection you can produce a quite distinctive style, even one that you can put your finger on and say was Japanese, Victorian, or whatever. Plants can be used to produce a focus of attention or to highlight some decorative element in a colour scheme or pattern that you wish to emphasize, or even to disguise or camouflage some ugly architectural feature of a room. With such versatility houseplants are an invaluable decorative accessory which will stimulate new and imaginative schemes.

In this carefully balanced interior the plants are a vital ingredient in completing the look. Each area has been considered and plants found to suit particular places.

A huge specimen of the palm Howeia forsteriana can't fail to make an important statement in any interior. The simple cream-coloured earthenware container highlights the palm and blends perfectly with the colour scheme of the room.

Centres of attraction

Every room needs a centre of attraction. It could be a beautiful floor rug or a special piece of furniture or just a stunning colour scheme. But very often a room is lacking just that something to set it off. Plants are the perfect answer for providing a focal point or emphasis – choose the right one and the room comes alive.

One enormous plant, such as a cissus allowed to grow to the ceiling, will create an impression by its sheer size, but it must be well-cared for and always look its best to be successful. A group of plants close together can be as effective and give more scope and choice by enabling you to replace varieties and subtly rearrange the grouping to give more decorative options. One large plant on its own has to be something you are really happy to live with for some time as it is quite a commitment in terms of time and money but if you make the right choice it can be well worthwhile. Decide whether your room needs a big solid-leaved plant such as a monstera or yucca. In contrast you might choose something more delicate such as *Ficus benjamina*, which can be bought as a small tree. A tall dizygotheca or palm would have a similar effect. *Howeia belmoreana* is a good palm species and has the advantage of surviving fairly low temperatures.

If you plan to keep the plant for a long time in one place make sure the conditions suit it and spend some time in choosing a container which complements the plant. In this situation it could be a good idea to invest in a self-watering trough as a large plant will need quite a bit of looking after, particularly in the summer months. A focus plant will probably be most needed in a living room or perhaps in a dining room or hall. Bear in mind the style and colour scheme of the room before deciding on a suitable plant. Although the plant is there to make a dramatic statement it shouldn't look at odds with its surroundings.

In a cool monochrome interior an arrangement of several plants together makes a stunning focus in an empty corner. The yuccas have been grouped in a very plain container and their differing heights add emphasis and interest. A small-leaved trailer infills at the base and softens any hard edges. An arrangement like this must be well cared for and always in tip-top condition to create the maximum impact possible.

Centrepoints

Many rooms these days lack a visual centre. People are reinstating the fireplace as a way of creating a focal point but there are still many houses having rooms with large areas of window, which although curtained and furnished, have an empty feel about them, especially at night. A plant has a way of adding life of its own to a room and used boldly, say in the very centre of a living room, on a low table, can do wonders for the visual appeal of the surroundings. A small room might be impractical for this central treatment but if not one beautiful plant isolated on its own table or on a plant stand in a corner or against a wall can still make an important statement. It could be a permanent choice of plant or could be changed regularly to suit the seasons.

There is usually one plant in a collection which excels itself or flowers spectacularly for a short time, coming into the limelight for a week or so. If you have spotlights this is the time to make full use of them and focus light onto the special plant. For dramatic effect your chosen plant should be in splendid isolation, so banish any others to different parts of the house, or group them elsewhere in the room well away from the focal one. Plants which would be ideal for this star treatment would be dramatic foliage subjects such as the peacock plant, croton or caladium which come in dozens of different colour variations now, or perhaps a flowering plant at its best such as an azalea or poinsettia. A group of several plants would also make a splendid centrepiece, but for maximum effect they should all be of the same variety and, if a flowering type, should preferably be of a single colour. A low basket

A brilliant splash of red in a neutral colour scheme. The colour creates emphasis, but in fact any plant would look special as a contrast to the plain surfaces and lack of pattern in this sophisticated interior. The plant is a hippeastrum.

container brimful with several African violets all in flower can be just as stunning as one big flowering plant. This is also a good chance to show off a more exotic type of plant, one which is difficult to fit in with other more homely ones. An orchid would be a good choice, or one of the bromeliad family, such as the marvellous pink-flowering urn plant. Experiment with a range of houseplants both foliage and flowering until you find what suits your room and really creates a centre of attraction.

Enhancing a room

Plants have a wonderful knack of not just enlivening a room but actually becoming useful decorative devices that make the most of good features or disguise the bad ones. Any room in a house can have things that need highlighting as well as lots of areas that you'd rather not draw too much attention to. Plants can work for you in solving difficult decorating problems and they are cheaper and a lot more fun than getting in the builders.

Many old houses which have seen years of changes and alterations, particularly to plumbing, may have tangles of pipe-work either exposed or badly boxed in. A hanging basket or container with a good easy trailing species such as an ivy or the grape ivy can disguise the ugliest bits and can even be trained along the parts you wish to hide. Town houses and flats often have windows looking out onto blank walls or dingy courtyards or simply have grey and uninspiring views. In cases like these it's best to forget what is outside and do a cover-up job in front of the window. A good way to completely fill a window is to fix narrow glass shelves across the whole area with a

A room with an ugly view can be transformed by grouping suitable plants in front of the offending window. Here a clever grouping on several levels has successfully blotted out an ugly building beyond. The Nephrolepis fern makes a perfect hanging basket plant as it grows into a spherical shape. Other plants such as the trailing ivy add interest right down to the floor level.

vertical spacing to suit your plants and then fill the shelves with greenery. Small baskets or hanging plant pots can be fixed to the window frame on either side and all the way down if you like, then filled with plants which trail or hang, covering as much glass as possible.

Rooms with enormously high ceilings can be made to appear much lower by hanging a row of baskets or special containers at a point in the room where they attract the eye and discourage you from looking higher. Ferns of all kinds make the right shapes for this treatment but aren't always the easiest plants to look after. Grape ivy, tradescantia

or *Philodendron scandens* are equally suitable and simpler to keep. Sometimes ceilings are simply hideous or in bad shape and then the basket treatment will disguise or blot out what you don't want to see when all else fails.

In an area where the floor covering changes from one type to another, say in a large open-plan living/dining room, the break can be softened by standing a group of large foliage plants at the side of the room where the two materials meet. They could be placed on both sides if necessary. This gives a softening effect and could also be used where wall coverings change abruptly.

A break between dining area and living area has been softened and disguised by the clever use of a screen, plus a really beautiful tall Ficus benjamina. It cleverly fills a redundant space in the room and adds great style at the same time.

Highlights

Above *This beautiful bay window has been purposely left without curtains or blinds and simply painted white. The plants and window mutually enhance each other. The window might look too stark without the softening effect of green foliage. The plain white window throws the plant into relief.*

Right *A pair of palms dramatically flank a simple central window.*

Most of us probably have more things that need hiding in our houses than need showing off but if you think positively about each room and try to find its good points you may be surprised at how many places there are where a plant would really accentuate an attractive feature. A pretty window with perhaps an arched frame or one which has shutters and is too good to hide behind curtains will benefit by having a plant hanging or standing in front of it. Something centrally placed will emphasize the fine proportions and symmetry of a window while a plant standing on either side will focus attention on a pretty or unusual shape, or on a special feature such as little leaded panes or stained glass. Plants near windows also draw the eye beyond into a garden so if your garden is worth more than the occasional glance a strategically placed green plant will lead you outside visually. If you are lucky enough to have a fine fireplace which deserves highlighting, a pair of matching plants flanking it will look spectacular. Something quite tall and formal such as two umbrella plants would look good beside a period fireplace and will thrive provided the

fireplace is unused. A more relaxing plant might be one of the ivy varieties. In summer a pair of standard fuchsias would look perfect. But remember fuchsias should not be kept indoors for more than two weeks.

Polished wood floors or shiny ceramic tiles are always worth making more of and a group of plants or one good foliage plant would perfectly complement their shiny surfaces. Green plants have a way of bringing wood to life, including polished furniture, so bear it in mind when choosing a surface to stand a plant on. Dark-coloured woods need the brightest, lightest greens whereas pale woods, such as new oak or ash, can take dark glossy leaves such as those of philodendrons or spathiphyllum. An arched recess, corner display shelves or similar architectural detail is an obvious and successful place to put a plant you wish to draw attention to. This is a chance to use a spectacular plant and one which makes a good silhouette. Choose something with good shape and plenty of space – not a dense mass of foliage – perhaps a plant which has an interesting leaf shape, such as one of the fern family or perhaps *Fatsia japonica* or its close relative ×*Fatshedera lizei*.

Screens and dividers

Plants can often be used to make screens or divide a room either visually or physically. There are many reasons why this might be desirable, not least because these days so many houses have a great deal of open-plan space. Many people take all their meals in one end of a kitchen but don't want always to look at the working end when eating. Bed-sits are perfect examples of living spaces that really benefit from plants positioned to break up areas used for so many different activities. A screen of plants between two areas looks good and, strangely, often adds to a feeling of space. If there is already a piece of furniture or work surface as the basis of a barrier then plants can be hung above in pots or baskets fixed to the ceiling, or maybe grouped on the surface, either at the sides or all the way along. You can always mix hanging and standing plants for the maximum flexibility. A really large room may be able to take a complete wall of greenery which can be turned into a fixture with a proper trough to take large plants,

Above A clever room divider made from a light wooden trellis covered with × Fatshedera lizei sits with asparagus fern at the base in a wooden trough.

Right A group of plants can make a versatile screen on a work top or chest of drawers. Containers all of the same material help hold the group together.

A sunny archway into a garden room is almost curtained by trails of foliage which gently filter the light. Plants might need a little help to get established across a doorway plus some unobtrusive tying-in to keep things under control. Between a conservatory and a sitting room the plants could be planted straight into the soil or otherwise provided with a really good-sized pot.

including some that will grow and twine upwards supported on a trellis or similar structure of this kind. Many rooms, even if they are not very large, benefit from the screening of one part from another, rather as one might do in a garden. Create a small tucked-away corner and the room begins to look larger than it really is.

All kinds of foliage plants can be used for making screens, but bear in mind that the middle of a very long room may be quite dark and will only support plants that can survive a low light level. Ivy, monstera, tradescantia, asparagus fern, climbing philodendrons, ferns, palms and many other foliage plants will be useful for making screens.

A large kitchen is also a good place for the screen treatment – so many plants thrive in the atmosphere. To keep as much work-top space clear as possible, suspend the plants in decorative rope hangers or pretty natural baskets. A conventional ceiling will have regularly spaced joists for fixing the strong hooks needed to carry the weight of a hanging plant.

Creating an atmosphere

An uncompromisingly modern flat needs stark shapes and strong outlines to add atmosphere. The cacti on the low glass and perspex table makes exactly the right effect.

When we choose colour schemes and furniture for our houses we are automatically creating an atmosphere. We may set out to copy or produce a particular style from scratch or we may have bought a house which already has a strong atmosphere of its own, a period home perhaps or a distinctive house designed and built to someone's requirements. Most of us, however, live in relatively new houses with little that makes them different from masses of others throughout the country. Conversion flats and modernised semis also vary little in essentials, all leaving us with much the same ingredients to play around with. Some people have strong views about their interior surroundings and spend a lot of time and money on achieving the perfect home. Others have neither the interest nor the money and furnish fairly haphazardly, buying things when they can be afforded or when something wears out. Every decision we make over the choice of carpet, curtains or

kitchen furnishings is inspired by something, even if we are unaware precisely of the influence. It may just be to do with comfort or price, but somewhere within us there is a basic feeling that we want to surround ourselves with what suits us for whatever reason.

It doesn't take an enormous bank balance or limitless time to create a home with atmosphere and it is really not much harder to pick the right colour first time than the wrong one. A home without plants or flowers loses a lot of atmosphere. A room with a living, growing, green plant in it feels alive itself and welcoming. Plants are one of the cheapest and easiest ways of adding colour and excitement to any room and even create an atmosphere of their own which wouldn't be there without them. Whether you have a room which already has a strong identity but which needs more emphasis, or a blank room which needs a style of its own, houseplants can be an easy and versatile solution to the problem.

This beautiful city flat would lose an enormous amount of atmosphere if the plants were taken away. The light airy foliage and fresh green colour provides contrast and texture in this subtly coloured interior.

Adding a sense of period

Starting with rooms which have great atmosphere, the trick is to use plants which work with existing features and not against them. A low-ceilinged, Elizabethan timber-framed house looks entirely wrong filled with palms, monsteras or other tropical plants. Simpler, softer subjects such as pelargoniums, cyclamen, begonias and ivies have much more the right feel and don't clash with the traditional atmosphere. Similarly a cool high-tech city interior might look very strange with small fussy plants; the scale and simplicity would demand plants which are large and dramatic and make bold statements themselves. This is a case for a beaucarnia or a big *Dracaena marginata* or an aphelandra, whose marvellous graphic markings remove any chance of it being ignored. A sunny summery room in any type of house could be made to feel like a conservatory by using plenty of bright green foliage and maybe hanging baskets at the windows. An old-fashioned wire plant stand could be put to proper use and stacked with ferns and other graceful plants and, to carry the theme further, furniture in the room could be made from wicker or cane or simply painted white and covered with a fresh green-and-white print fabric. A tiled or plain wood floor or pale carpet would complete the scheme perfectly, a particularly suitable solution for a dining or breakfast room.

Many people live in houses built in Victorian times and nowadays, thank goodness, most owners are keen to keep the original features, often going as far as to replace in the style of the period things which were removed in the days of boarding over and covering up. Many fabrics and wallpaper designs are suitable for this style of house, and furniture which fits in with the character is not difficult to find. Palms and ferns were great favourites with the Victorians as was the aspidistra, one of the few plants which could survive smoky polluted city air and gas fumes. They were so common in Victorian days that for a long time afterwards they were largely ignored. They are remarkably long lived and a good well-grown specimen, particularly one of the new variegated forms, looks magnificent in a

Far left A sophisticated Georgian drawing room needs elegant plants to emphasize its character. A tree-sized Ficus benjamina looks wonderful, framed by the floor-to-ceiling period window.

Left A cascade of foliage plants enforce the lush Edwardian feel of this lovely garden room.

decorative cachepot as the centrepiece to a Victorian-style living room.

The country-house style might sound far too grand for most of us but if your taste in furniture is traditional and includes loose-covered sofas and chairs with rugs on the floor then you may be part of the way there. Add an azalea or a bowlful of cyclamen and in the summer place a standard fuchsia near a window. Orange trees have just the right feel about them too, as does any plant which looks as if it has just come, beautifully cosseted, from the greenhouse. Scented-leaved pelargoniums are perfect and bowls full of flowering bulbs in winter create a feeling of tradition and comfort which with a little time and space is easy to copy. Pot your plants into old terracotta pots if you can find them – plastic looks completely out of place.

The sumptuous and exotic furnishings of this Eastern-inspired sitting-room need rather special plants. Palms have just the right combination of grace and flamboyance to work well with all the mirror, gilt and silk surfaces, without being too fussy.

Below and far right *Fabrics in an Indian and Middle-Eastern style have been used to decorate this sitting-room. It makes a stylish setting for cyclamens and begonias.*

The Eastern look

If your taste in interiors is simple and spare, influenced perhaps by the Japanese tradition, then choose your plants carefully and make them an important part of the complete scheme. The art of growing bonsai trees has recently become popular in this country but you can only expect to keep plants treated in this way indoors for short periods of time as they require normal outdoor seasonal weather conditions to really thrive. Grow instead a Japanese azalea or a soft-leaved plant such as *Philodendron bipinnatifidum* which has the look of a Japanese water-garden plant. Red flowers too seem to strike the right note, perhaps an *Anthurium scherzerianum* in flower or an Asiatic lily, or a single brilliant scarlet amaryllis. The Japanese love to use iris in their flower arrangements and any plant with tall narrow strap-shaped leaves would also provide the right effect. There are several plants to look out for such as *Rhoeo spathacea* or the narrower leaved dracaenas.

In complete contrast to the pared-down Eastern style, you may prefer more glamour and comfort, and nothing helps more towards a feeling of luxury and hedonism than flowers and plants with beautiful perfumes. Many of these appear throughout the book but a few with really spectacular scent are worth mentioning here. *Lilium regale*, which is one of the best lilies for pot culture, has a magnificent scent and so does L. *longiflorum*, another white one. On a warm summer evening they will scent the whole room. The stephanotis is also a highly scented plant and again has white flowers. Although it is probably best grown in a conservatory many houses will have conditions suitable for it. The jasmine commonly grown as a house-plant also has a powerful fragrance and, like the lily and the stephanotis, it has a wonderful exotic feel about it. There are many other plants which have lovely scents such as the hyacinth but somehow their fragrance is more homely and simple without the slightly mysterious overtones of the other three.

Back to simplicity and the simple country

feel of wood and brick and lots of fresh air. If you prefer Indian rugs, or dhurries, on waxed floors or deep-pile carpet and crisp cotton sheets to satin ones then your plants should look countrified too. Pelargoniums look right whether indoors or out and at one time few cottages didn't have their pot or two of cheerful flowers on a window-sill. Busy lizzies are another good old-fashioned sort of plant, often badly grown and allowed to get leggy and sparse. They do like plenty of light indoors but not direct sunlight and as they are really very easy to propagate from seed or cuttings there is no reason why you shouldn't have a regular supply to fill your window-sills. A plant often seen for sale in early summer and sometimes used outdoors is the Paris daisy or marguerite (*Chrysanthemum frutescens*). It is often grown as a pretty mop-headed standard. It is happy indoors and always looks fresh and bright with masses of simple white daisy flowers smothering the foliage. Black-eyed Susan is another countrified plant for the summer and during the winter months little pots of primroses can take over to provide very welcome colour. Foliage plants for a simple unsophisticated look might include the spider plant and all kinds of ivies, some of the smaller ferns and the beautifully easy piggy-back plant.

Finally if your fantasies run to tropical islands or steamy jungles then perhaps you could indulge them by making your own version in a suitable room. The bathroom might be a good place to begin, especially as a cunning use of mirrors here can increase the impact enormously. One or two really large and spectacular plants ideally placed

on a low shelf could set the scene with smaller ones grouped below or hung amongst them. A palm or a large monstera would give some height and if combined with a plant such as a schefflera with a good horizontal spread of leaves would provide an illusion of layers of the forest. A dizygotheca or schefflera maybe and then other foliage plants to fill in with such as philodendrons or ficus varieties. If the conditions are right perhaps an orchid or something as spectacular as a strelitzia could be stood to complete the setting. For this 'jungle' to thrive you must be careful not to allow the temperature to sink below 15°C (60°F) for any amount of time.

A neat and simple still-life made using a group of the plainest white ceramic pudding bowls and a bucket. The mirror-topped table gives you twice the picture and the plants have been carefully chosen for their contrasting shapes and styles. The black-and-white colour scheme might be too severe without the relief of green from plants and warmth from the pine floor.

Setting the scene

Planning a small display of houseplants for a special occasion or as a decorative highlight takes a little thought and imagination. The great secret in getting maximum effect is to concentrate on what you are good at and what succeeds for you, as well as on the way that you display things. Study magazine and book illustrations, window displays and exhibitions, where plants have been used decoratively. The chances are that no special or complicated techniques have been used, simply a knowledge of what looks right with what and a basic understanding of colour and form.

Grouping plants is discussed throughout the book but it is such an important idea when you are trying to get the biggest impact from small beginnings. Collect together a few small plants which have been dotted around the house and put them in a good-looking container, perhaps a basket or a ceramic bowl. Place them on a table or a low piece of furniture and, if you can, spotlight them. Try making a small landscape from mossy selaginellas in a low, rectangular tray or basket or march a row of tiny pots right across a dinner table. Choose something small for this such as helxine or African violets. Special occasions demand extra effort and there is no reason why you shouldn't include houseplants in the decoration. At Christmas time use a large foliage plant as the basis of a stunning focal point. You could tie glossy ribbons made into bows all over the plant, as large or small as you like. Keep to one colour for a sophisticated look or use brilliantly clashing colours or glittery bows for a really dazzling effect. You needn't stop at ribbons, try prettily wrapped sweets or presents, or tiny glass Christmas tree baubles and decorations. For a less seasonal version you could add artificial flowers to your plant, attaching them with the thinnest florist rose wire. The only thing to remember about this is to be gentle and don't weigh the branches down too heavily or tie the wire too tightly.

A hall is the first place that a visitor notices so for a party or any special occasion try to do something splendid as a welcoming sight for all your guests. A mixed bowl of plants, including a flowering plant or two, makes a special arrangement that will set the scene for the whole party. It might seem extravagant to buy plants especially for an event such as this but they do give much better value than the equivalent spent on fresh flowers and you have the bonus of enjoying them for a long time after the party. If guests are staying it is thoughtful to provide something in a guest bedroom. A scented plant such as a jasmine or a pot or two of primroses would be a beautiful surprise. In fact any flowering plant would be suitable as it need only be there for a short time. Something on a dressing or bedside table shows a lot of thought and cheers what can often be a rather cold and unlived-in looking room.

For a party, or Christmas, or any special occasion a plant, in this case a dwarf conifer, can be decorated with single blooms of artificial flowers. Each blossom can be attached very gently with fine florist's wire and removed when the event is over. There is a huge range of fabric flowers available at most florists and for maximum effect, as here, keep it simple and use one type and colour.

A large buffet meal spread out for a party needs some kind of decoration and it is fun to match the style of food or the way it is presented with plants. This is actually easier to do with plants than with fresh flowers as there is a far greater variety of shapes and forms to choose from. A simple lunch or supper with cheese and salads and maybe a single hot dish or soup could have its rustic theme carried through to pots of pelargoniums in baskets. They have just the right feel about them, especially if there is a gingham tablecloth spread across the table. A more elegant meal, say for a wedding or christening, would look marvellous with white cloth, plain china and pure white cyclamen or azaleas as the centre piece or, if the buffet is large, spaced at regular intervals along its length. To carry this idea even further, create a miniature Japanese garden with pebbles and plants and water for a *tempura* meal or cacti for a Mexican creation!

Right *A pretty grouping of plants plus tiny treasures and trinkets add enormously to this feminine, frilly room in plain almond green. The containers for the plants have been carefully chosen to add to the whole arrangement and the plants too are light and frothy looking. A small vase of cut flowers can add life and sparkle to a foliage grouping.*

A stylish all-blue dining-room is just the right setting for a summery lunch. What better to set it off than a mop-headed hydrangea in full bloom.

Aechmea fasciata

Aechmea fasciata
Urn plant
Height: 45-60cm (1½-2ft)
Spread: 38-45cm (15-18in)
Minimum winter temperature:
10-13°C (50-55°F).
Distinctive bromeliad forming
a vase-shaped rosette of wide,
stiff, grey-green leaves with
prickly edges. The leaves are
covered in a white fluff. A
flower stem grows from the
central vase during August and
lasts for several months.
Lime-free open-textured
compost is essential, and keep
the central vase topped up
with water. Also, ensure the
compost is moist, especially
when the plant is in flower. The
plant dies after flowering. New
shoots are produced at the
base.

Anthurium scherzerianum
Flamingo flower
Height: 23cm (9in)
Spread: 30-38cm (12-15in)
Minimum winter temperature:
16°C (60°F).

Anthurium scherzerianum

Stately flowering houseplant
with dark evergreen lance-
shaped leaves, up to 15cm
(6in) long, held on stiff but
splaying stems. Palette-
shaped, shiny bright red
spathes, with yellow, tail-like
centres are borne at leaf
height.
Good drainage and a compost
containing sphagnum moss
are essential. Divide crowded
plants in spring. Shade during
summer, moist but freely
draining compost and a
constant temperature are the
keys to success.

Calathea makoyana

Calathea makoyana
Peacock flower
Height: 45-60cm (1½-2ft)
Spread: 30-45cm (1-1½ft)
Minimum winter temperature:
13°C (55°F).
Stunningly beautiful foliage
houseplant with oval to
oblong silvery-green leaves,
10-15cm (4-6in) long. The main
veins are marked with dark-
green irregular elongated
blotches. The leaf edges are
green, while underneath the
leaf is zoned purple and red.
John Innes potting compost or
a peat-based type are both
suitable. Re-pot plants that
have out-grown their pots in
April. At this stage excessively
large plants can be divided.

Citrus mitis
Calamondin
also sold as
Citrus microcarpa
Height: 45cm (1½ft)
Spread: 38-45cm (15-18in)
Minimum winter temperature:
13°C (55°F).

Citrus mitis

A dwarf, neat, evergreen citrus
plant for the home, bearing
star-shaped, waxy-white
flowers 12mm (½in) wide and
richly fragrant. The walnut-
sized orange fruits are edible
but very sour. They can be
used for marmalade.
John Innes potting compost
suits it well, and a cool, not
too dry, atmosphere is
essential. Good light but not
direct sunlight is best and
avoid warm centrally heated
rooms. It is a difficult plant to
care for.

Dracaena deremensis
Height: 90cm-1.2m (3-4ft)
Spread: 38cm (15in)
Minimum winter temperature:
13°C (55°F).
A distinctive evergreen foliage
houseplant. It has a tuft of
broad, strap-like glossy-green
leaves with silver stripes.

Dracaena deremensis

Several forms are offered for
sale, such as 'Warneckei' with
distinctive white stripes down
the edges of the leaves, and
'Bausei' with a white stripe
down the centre.
Dracaena draco, the Dragon tree,
has a palm-like habit, with a
cluster of sword-like mid-green
leaves in a cluster at its top.
Dracaena sanderiana has leaves
with wavy edges, grey-green
with cream to silvery
contrasting edges.
John Innes potting compost
suits it. Keep the compost
relatively dry during winter
when the plants are not
growing rapidly. Give more
water during summer.

Dracaena terminalis

Dracaena terminalis
Flaming dragon/Ti plant
correctly known as
Cordyline fruticosa,
but also called
Cordyline terminalis
Height: 45-75cm (1½-2½ft)
Spread: 30-38cm (12-15in)
Minimum winter temperature:
13°C (55°F).
Beautiful foliage houseplant
with mid to deep-green lance-
shaped leaves growing from a
central point. The leaves are
variously flushed with red,
purple or cream.
John Innes potting compost
suits it well; re-pot if need be
in late spring. Tourists abroad
are often sold stems of this
plant called Ti logs, and

sometimes these are also available in Britain. These logs can be rooted by planting them in an open compost, keeping them warm, in shade and moist.

Dizygotheca elegantissima

Dizygotheca elegantissima
False aralia
previously sold as
Aralia elegantissima
Height: 1.2-1.5m (4-5ft)
Spread: 38-45cm (15-18in)
Minimum winter temperature:
 13°C (55°F).
Graceful, rather elegant foliage houseplant with a central, stiff, erect stem from which radiates stems bearing seven to ten narrow, spider-like, coppery-red leaves in a palm fashion. Later the leaves change to a deep olive-green.
A well-lit position is preferred but shield it from intense sunlight.

Ficus elastica 'Decora'
Rubber plant
India-rubber plant
Height: 1.2-1.8m (4-6ft)
Spread: 60-75cm (2-2½ft)
Minimum winter temperature:
 16°C (61°F).
This plant has a central stem with oblong to oval shiny dark-green leaves, up to 30cm (1ft) long. Several forms are available such as *Ficus elastica* 'Doescheri' with pale-green leaves and ivory and pink

variegations. *Ficus elastica* 'Schryveriana' has cream variegations and *Ficus elastica* 'Tricolor' has cream and pink variegations.
Lower leaves will drop off if over watered.

Ficus lyrata
Fiddle-leaf fig
also known as
Ficus pandurata
Height: 1.2-1.5m (4-5ft)
Spread: 38-45cm (15-18in)
Minimum winter temperature:
 16°C (61°F).
Foliage plant with large, glossy, dark-green fiddle-shaped leaves with wavy edges.

Ficus lyrata

John Innes potting compost is suitable. Position in good but diffused sunlight during summer.

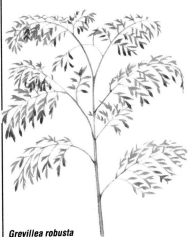

Grevillea robusta

Grevillea robusta
Silky oak
Height: 90cm-1.8m (3-6ft)
Spread: 38-45cm (15-18in)
Minimum winter temperature:
 5°C (41°F).
A large, distinctive foliage houseplant with finely divided deep green feathery leaves, pale bronze when young, attractively covered with silky hairs.
John Innes potting compost is suitable. Water freely during summer, but sparingly in winter.

Haworthia margaritifera
Height: 7.5cm (3in)
Spread: 10-13cm (4-5in)
Minimum winter temperature:
 5°C (41°F).
Attractive small succulent houseplant, ideal for a window-ledge. It has distinctive rosettes of dark green, lance-shaped leaves, formed in a broad rosette and covered with white, raised spots. From June it bears greenish-white flowers, but the plant is primarily grown for its attractive leaves.
Well-drained compost and a position in partial or full sun is needed.

Heptapleurum arboricola

Heptapleurum arboricola
also known as
Schefflera arboricola
Height: 1.8m (6ft)
Spread: 60-90cm (2-3ft)

Minimum winter temperature:
 10°C (50°F).
Large foliage plant (though it can be kept smaller) with branching stems. It bears hand-shaped leaves formed of nine, glossy green narrow leaflets.
John Innes potting compost is suitable, but keep it moist during summer. Slight shade is also needed. Re-pot during April.

Hippeastrum – hybrids
Amaryllis
Height: 30-45cm (1-1½ft)
Spread: 15-20cm (6-8in)
Minimum winter temperature:
 13°C (55°F).

Hippeastrum

Spectacularly flowered bulbs, displaying up to four funnel-shaped flowers, 10-13cm (4-5in) wide, in a range of colours – white, pink, rose, red and scarlet – and usually bought to flower at Christmas or spring. The mid- to deep-green leaves are long and strap-like, the flowers being borne on one or two stiff upright stems.
Large bulbs are planted singly in pots during September and October to flower from February onwards; specially-prepared bulbs will flower at Christmas. John Innes potting compost is suitable. Leave half the bulb exposed and water thoroughly. Keep the compost slightly moist until the shoots appear when the amount of water can be increased.
Bottom heat encourages the formation of roots.

Howeia belmoreana

Howeia belmoreana
also known as
Kentia belmoreana
Height: 2.4-3m (8-10ft)
Spread: 1.8-2.4m (6-8ft)
Minimum winter temperature:
7-10°C (45-50°F).
Delightful palm with dark-green leaves, 45cm (1½ft) long and 30cm (1ft) across, formed of many narrow, serrated leaflets drooping gracefully from the central mid-rib.
John Innes potting compost is suitable, and keep moist during summer. If possible, position in a light area during winter. Can be kept in a sheltered patio after danger of frosts has passed.

Howeia fosteriana

Howeia fosteriana
also known as
Kentia fosteriana
Height: 2.4-3m (8-10ft)
Spread: 1.8-2.4m (6-8ft)
Minimum winter temperature:
7-10°C (45-50°F).
Eye-catching graceful palm, distinguished from *Howeia belmoreana* in having fewer leaflets.
Treat as for *Howeia belmoreana*.

Hyacinthus orientalis
Common hyacinth
Height: 15-23cm (6-9in)
Spread: 7.5-10cm (3-4in)
Minimum winter temperature:
7°C (45°F).
Well-known bulbous plants that produce 10-15cm (4-6in) candles of fragrant flowers during Christmas and into spring in a wide range of colours, including white, pink, red, yellow and blue.
They can be bought in bud ready to be brought inside to a cool room where they will last in flower for several weeks. Alternatively, gift-packs of the bulbs, pots and compost are sold in early autumn, and it is not difficult to plant your own.

Iris reticulata
Height: 13-15cm (5-6in)
Spread: 7.5cm (3in)
Minimum winter temperature:
10°C (50°F).
An easily grown bulbous iris with 6.5-7.5cm (2½-3in) wide, purple-blue flowers with golden markings, appearing in February and March.
During autumn pot up the bulbs close together in John Innes potting compost, covering their tips well. Water and place in a cool, vermin-proof place for eight to ten weeks, then bring into a temperature of 10°C (50°F) to flower. *Iris danfordiae*, with honey-scented vivid yellow flowers, can also be treated in the same way. Do not subject either of these bulbs to high temperatures. Feed during active leaf growth.

Jasminum polyanthum

Jasminum polyanthum
Pink jasmine
Height: 1.5-3m (5-10ft)
Climber
Minimum winter temperature:
7°C (45°F).
Jasmine is best grown in a greenhouse where it can be given a permanent framework for support. In the home young plants can be trained over a 45-60cm (1½-2ft) high loop of wire or pliable canes.
Do not feed or give it too high a temperature or a very large pot as it may then produce masses of foliage at the expense of flowers.

Lilium 'Enchantment'
Height: 90cm-1.2m (3-4ft)
Spread: 30-38cm (12-15in)
Minimum temperature:
16°C (61°F)
Attractive mid-century hybrid lily that can be gently forced into early flower. It has outward-facing, cup-shaped, bright red flowers, often 15cm (6in) wide. Other lilies for pot planting include the Easter lily, *Lilium longiflorum*, with its delightfully fragrant, white trumpet-shaped 13-15cm (5-6in) long flowers and golden pollen; the Golden-rayed lily, *Lilium auratum*, again with white, highly fragrant flowers, this time bowl-shaped and 25-30cm (10-12in) wide. They have purple spots on the inner surface. *Lilium regale* is another candidate, displaying fragrant white, funnel-shaped flowers, 10-13cm (4-5in) long.
As soon as the bulbs are available in autumn they should be potted well down in John Innes potting compost, either one to a 15cm (6in) pot or three to a larger one and left in a cool place to encourage root formation. Keep the compost moist. When shoots appear bring indoors to a cool room, increasing the temperature when the buds are fully developed to 18°C (65°F)

Pelargonium
Height: see below
Minimum winter temperature:
7-10°C (45-50°F).
These well-known houseplants produce magnificent flowers or attractive foliage, or both. Several types are grown. Zonal pelargoniums, often called geraniums and so confused with the hardy border geranium, have rounded mid-green leaves marked with bold and contrasting zones of chocolate-brown. Their flowers are single or double, and are borne in rounded heads from May to October. Most grow 30-45cm (1-1½ft) in their first year, eventually much higher, while miniature types are 15-23cm (6-9in) high. Regal pelargoniums have pale-green serrated leaves, with a more triangular shape. The pink to purple flowers, often 4-5cm (1½-2in) wide, are borne in heads on stems arising from the upper leaf-joints from May to October on plants 38-60cm (15-24in) high. Ivy-leaved pelargoniums (*Pelargonium peltatum*) have a trailing form, often with stems up to 60cm (2ft) or more long, and mid-green ivy-like leaves. Carmine-pink flowers appear from summer to autumn.
Scented-leaved pelargoniums are grown for their delightfully scented leaves; there are many varieties available.

Philodendron bipinnatifidum

Philodendron bipinnatifidum
Tree philodendron
Height: 90cm-1.2m (3-4ft)
Spread: 90cm-1m (3-3½ft)
Minimum winter temperature:
  13°C (55°F).

A non-climbing, relatively compact foliage plant, initially bearing heart-shaped leaves. Later, as the plant matures, the foliage becomes three lobed and increasingly more deeply incised. Fully grown leaves can be more than 45cm (1½ft) long.
Peat-based compost suits it well. Keep the compost well watered during summer and slightly moist the rest of the year.

Pteris cretica

Pteris cretica
Ribbon fern
Height: 30-38cm (12-15in)
Spread: 23-30cm (9-12in)
Minimum winter temperature:
  7°C (45°F).

A widely grown fern with light-green strap-shaped fronds. The most appealing forms are those with variegated or crested fronds, such as *Pteris cretica* 'Albolineata', which has a central white band running along each pinnae; and *Pteris cretica* 'Wilsonii' with crested tips to the fronds.
Position variegated forms out of direct light and water them freely during summer, but with some restraint the rest of the year.

Rhoeo spathacea

Rhoeo spathacea
Boat lily
Moses in the cradle
often sold as
Rhoeo discolor
Height: 20-30cm (8-12in)
Spread: 20-30cm (8-12in)
Minimum winter temperature:
  10°C (50°F).

Distinctive foliage houseplant, initially displaying a rosette of strap-shaped, fleshy, dark green leaves with purplish undersides. Later a short, thickened stem appears. The common name Boat lily is derived from the boat-shaped purple bracts surrounding the white flowers which may appear at any time of year. A variegated form is available, with cream stripes down the entire length of the leaves.
John Innes potting compost or a peat-based compost are suitable. Position out of strong, direct sunlight.

Rhoicissus rhomboidea
Grape ivy
Height: 1.2-1.8m (4-6ft)
Climber
Minimum winter temperature:
  7°C (45°F).

Well-known climbing foliage houseplant with glossy dark-green leaves formed of three leaflets, each irregularly diamond-shaped with toothed edges. The young leaves are smothered with brownish hairs.
The form *Rhoicissus rhomboidea* 'Jubilee' bears larger leaves and is much more vigorous and best restricted to entrance halls.
John Innes potting compost suits it well. Position in good light during winter. Do not over-water.

Schefflera actinophylla
Umbrella tree
now correctly
Brassaia actinophylla
Height: 1.8-2.1m (6-7ft)
Spread: 60-90cm (2-3ft)
Minimum winter temperature:
  10°C (50°F).

Schefflera actinophylla

Large, tree-like foliage houseplant with a single stem bearing stems with spear-shaped, glossy mid-green leaves borne in an umbrella-like arrangement.
John Innes potting composts suit it well; re-pot as necessary in spring. Large pots encourage more rapid growth but, even so, at no time is growth fast. It thrives in a well lit position out of direct sun rays. Do not allow the compost to become dry.

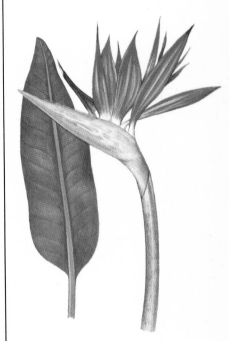

Strelitzia reginae

Strelitzia reginae
Bird of paradise flower
Height: 90cm-1.2m (3-4ft)
Spread: 90cm (3ft)
Minimum winter temperature:
  10°C (50°F).

A tender, clump-forming evergreen plant best suited to a greenhouse, but frequently sold for the home where eventually it will need a 25cm (10in) pot. The mid-green, bluntly spear-shaped leaves are surmounted during April and May by boat-shaped, purple-flushed green bracts housing orange-blue flowers. These very much resemble a bird.
John Innes potting compost suits it, and although the plant has a tropical appearance it is far hardier than often thought. Plants less than four or five years of age from seed seldom flower.

PLANTS OF CHARACTER

Houseplants are not simply collections of green leaves or flowers and leaves. Each variety has a very definite character, either due to its colour and habit, or because of its associations of place, or the feelings it may give us. Some plants are definitely exotic because of their foreign nature. Others have an aura that is much more difficult to pin down – elegance or flamboyance. These emotive plants can set a sense of style and mood that will give a distinct atmosphere to any room. To help you choose which might suit you, here is a collection of the various characters plants can assume.

Plants come in all shapes, sizes and colours and mix happily together. Here cyclamen, azalea, begonia and an African violet are shown off beautifully by a selection of different foliage plants – a fern, spider plant and a maranta.

Flamboyant

A room which is as brave as this in style and mix of colours can take a striking plant. The brilliant scarlet is echoed through the room in the cushions and the large painting.

A flamboyant plant is bright, elaborate and draws attention to itself and its surroundings; it cannot be overlooked. It is to be used when a bold stroke is needed and you want to make a strong point. Many flowering plants tend to fall into this category but only a few foliage ones, as flamboyance has more to do with colour than with form. The hippeastrum (Amaryllis belladonna) could definitely be termed flamboyant as it is so tall and striking, even in its delicate pale-pink colour variation. The bright yellow lily 'Connecticut King' or the vivid orange-lily 'Enchantment' are certainly flamboyant compared with the white varieties and a large specimen of a regal pelargonium in scarlet or crimson can be stunning, as can a gloxinia. Some flowering cacti perfectly fit this category and a well-grown Christmas cacti (Schlumbergera × buckleyi) in flower has the brightest and most translucent pink flowers you can imagine. A large-flowered azalea can look very flamboyant whereas the smaller-flowered hardy kinds are far more subtle and restrained. Anthurium scherzerianum has very plain glossy leaves but produces bright heart-shaped 'flowers' or spathes held above the foliage. The variety most commonly seen is this one with scarlet spathes.

Calceolarias are very definitely flamboyant, if not verging on the vulgar sometimes, but are useful when a really strong yellow, red or orange colour is needed in an interior. The Kaffir lily (Clivia miniata) is very striking when in flower rather in the way that an amaryllis is, although the Clivia's flowers are smaller. Finally there are some foliage plants with brilliant coloured leaves such as the croton Codiaeum variegatum pictum.

Dramatic

Drama means movement, excitement and the ability to capture one's imagination. Some plants have this quality naturally while others may need a bit of help in the way we display them and bring them to life. Although a dramatic plant may be brightly coloured, the most important attribute is habit; it has to have an eye-catching shape and growth form.

There may be many cases when a room

needs a touch of theatre to pull a decorative scheme together or liven up a blank area.

The yucca is a good candidate. The leaves shoot out from the stem like an explosion, making a bold splashy shape. It is especially effective when seen in silhouette. Ideally it needs a plain, uncluttered background to show it at its best. Large, older plants sometimes branch from the base making the whole shape bushier but usually they are grown from a single stout woody stem with a burst of two or three clumps of foliage from the top few centimetres. A pair of tall yuccas flanking a door or piece of furniture can look splendid as they are at their best in isolation away from other foliage plants.

Dracaena marginata tricolor is a stunningly dramatic plant. It has narrow knife-like leaves, striped green, cream and pink and, as in the yucca, the leaves burst out from the

centre of the plant. There is also the species D. *marginata* which has the foliage clustered at the top of a stem. The croton definitely belongs in this category, but needs some cosseting to really flourish. It needs constant warmth and no chills, plus humidity and plenty of light. Given all this it will reward you with amazing splashes of colour on its broad densely packed leaves. The veining varies from cream through yellow to red according to the individual cultivar. Certain cacti can be very dramatic especially if placed in a situation which makes the most of their extraordinary shapes and weird textures.

Any plant which is larger than average can provide drama but care has to be taken for the room not simply to look dwarfed by a monster. One plant which is difficult to place successfully is the sansevieria or mother-in-law's tongue. It has great style of its own but so often ends up looking tired and neglected on a window-sill. The variety 'Laurentii' has a creamy-yellow edge to the leaf and is far more dramatic than the plain green kind. Very often a row of several sansevieria plants together has greater impact than one alone. They seem to need a busy background to throw their simple shapes into relief. If their surroundings are too plain their visual strength seems to be diluted.

Left *This version of the pineapple, Ananas sagenaria 'striatus', can't fail to attract attention. Even without the central red flower it would be very dramatic.*

Below *A pair of tall-stemmed yuccas flanking a simple arched doorway add a sense of drama to a spacious yet rustic interior.*

Orchids add instant glamour and mystery to the simplest room. In this bathroom they add colour to a pale decorative scheme and a luxurious and exotic feel. Some kinds, such as the caladiums, are not difficult to grow and flower for weeks. They could be moved to other surroundings after flowering.

Exotic and Mysterious

The word exotic means foreign or outlandish and implies an air of strangeness and mystery. Many of the plants we would describe as exotic come from parts of the world we at one time knew very little about, and in some cases still do. Many live in climates that are radically different from ours and have developed forms and shapes that are quite different from our own native plants or at least from the majority of them. In the equatorial forests, for example, because of the hot humid climate, there is a far greater range of plant life than in temperate latitudes. There are epiphytes, those that grow and receive nourishment from other plants; carnivorous plants, such as the sundews and pitcher plants which trap and feed off insects, and plants with aerial roots which hang down from their stems. Although there are examples of carnivorous plants and epiphytes to be found in temperate latitudes, they are not plentiful and have always been thought of as rather odd and a bit different from 'normal' plants as can be seen from the stories that surround plants such as the mistletoe.

First on our list of indoor exotica must be orchids. These grow all over the world in the wild and many are native to the British Isles. But the types grown as indoor plants today are modern hybrid orchids bred from tropical species and are far removed from the orchids of chalk hills and beech woods.

Some grow to great size with flower spikes a metre long while others are fairly small and will sit happily on a narrow window-sill. The flowers themselves are often very complex in their colours and patterns, having often evolved to mimic insects, although the basic arrangement of petals never alters. The cymbidium type of orchids are usually suggested for beginners to grow and are easy but need space.

The bromeliads are another rather strange and exotic group of plants. They all tend to produce a central vase of leaves with no stems. The leaves are often striped and patterned, and beautifully coloured. The flowers are usually not at all like our idea of a conventional flower. *Aechmea fasciata* has a strange spiky pink flower held stiffly above greyish green leaves. The billbergia species are also in the bromeliad family and the pineapple or ananas family has lots of very striking variations in foliage types and can't fail to look exotic in any setting.

Bonsai or dwarfed trees and shrubs are becoming increasingly popular in this country, but are not really houseplants. They are simply tiny versions of normal trees and need outdoor conditions, but they can be brought in for short periods as part of a special display and then returned to dappled light in a sheltered situation outside. Other exotica include the gardenia which is really best in a cool greenhouse or conservatory and the beautifully scented hoya.

Bonsai plants have a mysterious feel to them – and a great history too. This dwarfed juniper is fine indoors for a short time but shoud be left outside for most of the year. Once you own one you may get hooked on the art of bonsai.

Palms always add style and elegance to any interior. The most commonly grown indoor form is Howeia forsteriana. When it reaches about this size it makes a perfect floor-standing specimen. The wicker-basket container works well in this situation but any large, simple container would look good. In a period setting an elaborate cachepot would look particularly fine.

Elegant and Stately

A truly elegant plant has a restrained habit of growth and a graceful outline with, ideally, beautifully curving stems. It may be simple in its shape but never dull; it should be definitely stylish and rather understated. Plants in this category blend easily with furnishings and subtly echo shapes or colours – never shout them down. Many rooms need the important element which foliage and cool colours give to them but don't need a bold statement in colour or shape. All white flowers have this undeniable elegance so go for white if you have a choice and want to add a touch of class. Pure white lilies have great romance and elegance and at last seem more widely available as houseplants. They are very easy to grow from bulbs and as long as you are organised enough to plant your bulbs at intervals between late winter and spring you can have a succession of flowering plants to bring indoors throughout the summer.

Tree-sized versions of foliage plants such as *Ficus benjamina* are very elegant although whatever size this plant is grown it has a stylish and delicate look about it. The leaves droop slightly and there is always space around each leaf and they never produce a confused effect as do some plants. Other elegantly leaved plants include schefflera, spathiphyllum and *Dizygotheca elegantissima*. The *Citrus microcarpa* is attractive in all stages of its flowering and fruiting and conjures up visions of 18th-century orangeries and grand houses. It prefers to be kept in cool surroundings such as a porch, conservatory or a light room with little or no heat.

Palms definitely invoke a feeling of grace and stateliness wherever they are placed. One of the taller varieties is *Howeia belmoreana* which can grow too tall for the average room but certainly adds atmosphere if you can give it space. *Howeia forsteriana* is usually planted with several plants in one pot and never reaches its potential height and is

therefore suitable for many homes. Its branches are very graceful and it makes a
splendid focal point in any room but visually
it is quite a busy-looking plant; it definitely
won't merge into the background. Finally

many varieties of plants which have
variegated types gain great elegance from
their colouring. Variegated ivies for example
have a lightness and style very different from
the plain green outdoor type.

*Cool white flowers, such
as Lilium grandiflora,
always look elegant.
This lily, now often sold
as a pot plant will add
style and a magical
scent to a room for a
few weeks, and can be
kept to flower again the
following year.*

Tranquility

Tranquility is perhaps one of the most difficult atmospheres to create; it is very much in the mind and the eye of the beholder. In any room, though, greenery will go a long way to making a soothing and tranquil effect. The colour simply cools and quietens its surroundings. Simply filling a room with foliage plants will not necessarily make for a gentle and soothing atmosphere. Plants can have bold and exciting shapes and dramatic forms of growth. Spiky upward-shooting leaves and branches tend to excite the eye rather than calm it and many plants have confused and busy leaf shapes and patterns to which one's eye is drawn. For a really soothing and tranquil setting aim for largish areas of green with not too much variation in shape and texture, and plants which have small neat leaves or large plain ones. Trailing and hanging plants, such as *Philodendron scandens*, are perfect too and

A wonderful showy display of white orchid blossom in a sophisticated city flat. Anything other than white would spoil the elegance of this interior and confuse the complicated colour scheme.

many of the fern species strike the right note with their cool shades of green and simple leaf shapes and soft habit of growth. They remind us of outdoors and shady places.

Pale-blue flowers also have a way of soothing although there are few plants which have this particular colouration. Morning glory (*Ipomoea tricolor*) has deep blue flowers but *Plumbago capensis* has just the right pale blue of a clear summer sky. Blue hydrangeas as well as the white versions, which are often tinged with green, are beautifully cooling and soothing to live with. Other white flowers that have the same effect are *Jasminum polyanthum*, with its delicious scent, and white cyclamen which have a very different beauty compared with their brilliant pink and red counterparts.

Ferns definitely have a tranquil aura which is hard to match and there are now many different types which are happy to live indoors. They do need protection from direct sunlight and need moisture round their roots. They will not stand a very dry atmosphere. A spray mister is useful for treating the foliage occasionally with tepid water. Plunging fern pots into larger containers which are filled with a material such as damp peat, or standing on a tray of damp pebbles will fulfil the fern's root moisture requirements. A large well-grown specimen of *Nephrolepis exaltata* looks magnificent in a hanging basket or as a focal point standing on a plant display stand. Ferns are happily grouped together and make a cool lush area of green in a dull corner.

A soothing white and neutral interior feels even more tranquil with a large amount of restful green foliage. This pretty drooping bamboo plant is neither too busy nor dramatic but gently brings some outdoor qualities indoors to brilliant effect.

Ananas sagenaria 'Striatus'
Red pineapple
Height: 45-60cm (1½-2ft)
Spread: 38-45cm (15-18in)
Minimum winter temperature: 16°C (61°F).
A beautiful bromeliad having long, strap-like, spiny-edged, grey-green shiny leaves with creamy-white edges. It also bears tightly clustered red flowers, although botanically they are really bracts.
Do not allow the compost to dry out when the plant is in growth, and water only sparingly at other times. Re-pot in early spring.

Astrophytum myriostigma
Bishop's cap cactus
Height: 15-20cm (6-8in)
Spread: 13-15cm (5-6in)
Minimum winter temperature: 5°C (41°F).

Astrophytum myriostigma

A globular cactus that with age assumes a cylindrical appearance with five or six prominently-veined ribs on a grey body, covered with white scales. From June to August it displays 4cm (1½in) wide pale yellow flowers.
Well-drained compost is essential, as well as a position in good light. Re-pot in spring.

Billbergia nutans
Angel's tears or Queen's tears
Height: 38-45cm (15-18in)
Spread: 38-45cm (15-18in)
Minimum winter temperature: 2°C (35°F) for short periods only.
Elegantly distinctive evergreen houseplant with erect, narrow, grass-like, serrated leaves that often droop at their tips. Displays pendulous short-lived 7.5-10cm (3-4in) flower clusters formed of large pink bracts surrounding green flowers edged with blue and possessing golden-yellow stamens.

Billbergia nutans

Another attractive type is the hybrid B*illbergia* × 'Windii' with wider leaves and 2.5-4cm (1-1½in) long and drooping flowers.
Well-drained lime-free soil and a humid atmosphere are essential. Divide and re-pot large plants in spring.

Calceolaria × herbeohybrida
Slipper flower
Height: 23-45cm (9-18in)
Spread: 20-38cm (8-15in)
Minimum winter temperature: 7°C (45°F).
Eye-catching half-hardy biennial houseplant with pouch-shaped flowers, 5-6.5cm (2-2½in) long, lasting from

Calceolaria

Christmas to early summer. They appear in shades of yellow, orange and red, spotted or blotched in contrasting colours.
Buy in bud, when they are just showing colour, and keep in a cool, shaded position, away from direct sunlight. Do not excessively water the compost or allow it to dry out.

Cleistocactus strausii
Silver torch cactus
Height: 90cm-1.2m (3-4ft)
Spread: 5-7.5cm (2-3in)
Minimum winter temperature: 5°C (41°F).
A beautiful columnar cactus, forming long, upright pillars with up to twenty-five shallow ribs, between which are areoles possessing white wool and thirty or more white spines. During July and August it displays 7.5cm (3in) long, red, tubular flowers.
Well-drained compost and good light are essential.

Clivia miniata
Kaffir lily
Height: 38-45cm (15-18in)
Spread: 45-50cm (18-20in)
Minimum temperature: 2°C (36°F).

Clivia miniata

A fleshy-rooted plant – best in a greenhouse or conservatory – with arching, glossy, dark green strap-like leaves. From March to August it has heads of trumpet-shaped orange-red flowers, borne on stout stems. John Innes potting compost is suitable, with the plants set in 20-25cm (8-10in) pots. Higher temperatures than those suggested above will encourage earlier flowering.

Cryptanthus bromelioides

Cryptanthus bromelioides
'Tricolor'
Height: 30-38cm (12-15in)
Spread: 20-25cm (8-10in)
Minimum winter temperature: 16°C (61°F).
A relatively upright bromeliad with mid-green spine-edged, leathery leaves with white, rose and creamy-yellow longitudinal stripes.
An open-textured, free-draining compost is essential. Keep it well watered when the plant is in growth.

Epiphyllum × ackermannii
Height: 60-90cm (2-3ft)
Spread: 20-38cm (8-15in)
Minimum winter temperature: 5°C (41°F).
These well-known large-flowered cacti, often with bell-shaped flowers up to 15cm (6in) wide, have flattened stems with wavy edges. There are many hybrids, mainly in red, white or yellow. The flowers appear during May and June. They survive quite low temperatures, although a few degrees higher than those suggested above ensures more flowers.
Peat-based composts suit them. Position in slightly diffused light.

Euphorbia splendens
Crown of thorns
also sold as
Euphorbia milii
Height: 30-45cm (1-1½ft)
Spread: 30-38cm (12-15in)
Minimum winter temperature: 5°C (41°F).

An instantly recognizable semi-succulent shrub for the home, with hard, prickly stems,

Euphorbia splendens

sparsely covered with pear-shaped mid-green leaves. Flowers may occur at any time, but mostly during winter, and are recognizable by the two kidney-shaped bracts that extend below them. Well-drained compost and a position in full sun is essential. Re-pot in May.

Ipomoea violacea
Morning glory
syns. *Ipomoea rubro-caerulea*
Ipomoea tricolor
Height: 1.5-2.1m (5-7ft), climber

Ipomoea violacea

Minimum temperature: 18°C (64°F), for seed germination in spring.
The beautiful red-purple to blue flowers of this climber need little description. It is normally grown as an annual. Several forms are available, but perhaps the best known is still *Ipomoea violacea* 'Heavenly Blue', with vivid-blue convolvulus-like flowers. Sow seed in March or April in John Innes potting compost, reducing the temperature as soon as germination has occurred. Keep the seedlings away from draughts, and give a position in good light.

Neoregelia carolinae

Neoregelia carolinae
Height: 25-30cm (10-12in)
Spread: 20-25cm (8-10in)
Minimum winter temperature: 16°C (61°F).
Well-known bromeliad with strap-like, leathery, bright green leaves with pointed tips. At flowering time, chiefly during summer, the central rosette turns bright red and a flower-head bearing violet-purple flowers appears. A commonly-grown form is *Neoregelia carolinae* 'Tricolor', which has bright green leaves striped creamy-yellow. At flowering time the whole plant assumes a pink flush. Well-drained compost is needed with plenty of water given during growing and flowering times.

Sansevieria trifasciata
Mother-in-law's tongue
Height: 45cm (1½ft)
Spread: 15-20m (6-8in)
Minimum winter temperature: 10°C (50°F).
Easily recognised foliage plant with erect, sword-like, sharply-pointed dark-green leaves, irregularly mottled with grey bands. The most attractive form is *Sansevieria trifasciata* 'Laurentii' which has thick creamy-yellow edges to the leaves.
John Innes potting compost or a peat-based type are suitable. Take care not to allow them to dry out.

Sinningia speciosa
Gloxinia
Height: 25cm (10in)
Spread: 25-30cm (10-12in)
Minimum winter temperature: 18°C (64°F).
May to August flowering, tender tuberous-rooted houseplant famed for its large, open-trumpet-shaped flowers in rich violets, purple and reds, and often spotted. The almost stemless dark-green velvety leaves are another delight. There are many named varieties.
The plants are usually bought in bud and if given the above temperature and a shady position will thrive.
Dormant tubers can be started into growth in February, but will require a high temperature, 21°C (70°F). Set the tubers close together in boxes of moist peat, and pot the tubers individually into pots when the growths are 5cm (2in) high.

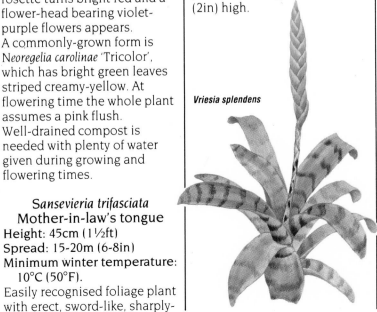

Vriesia splendens

Vriesia splendens
Flaming sword
Height: 30-45cm (1-1½ft)
Spread: 15-20cm (6-8in)
Minimum winter temperature: 18°C (64°F).
Spectacular eye-catching bromeliad with slender, dark-green leaves, beautifully marked with purple bands across the leaf. During late summer it produces a long, flattened, sword-shaped stem supporting yellow flowers surrounded by red bracts. John Innes potting compost is suitable. Water the compost freely from spring to autumn, but sparingly the rest of the year. Re-pot in spring.

Yucca elephantipes

Yucca elephantipes
Spineless yucca
Height: 60cm-1.2m (2-4ft)
Spread: 30-38cm (12-15in)
Minimum winter temperature: 7°C (45°F).
It is the young plants of this tropical stout-branched and stemmed tree that are grown in pots. They display long, sword-like, glossy-green, sharply-pointed leaves with slightly toothed edges. Another species often grown is *Yucca aloifolia*. They are also known as the Dagger plant or Spanish-bayonet. It is similar to the Spineless yucca. John Innes potting composts suit them. Water generously during summer but be restrained in the winter.

TOLERANT PLANTS

Finding a plant to suit every situation in the house might sound impossible; so few rooms have the perfect environment. If we have a few failures we tend to become discouraged. However there are dozens of plants which are quite happy in extreme conditions from hot and dry to dark and humid and there are many easy plants which are not in the least bit fussy about where they live. Sort out your problem areas and you will find there are plants which will make the most of them.

A tin-can warrior stands guard over this group of houseplants, containing something ideally suited for almost every spot in a house.

Bathrooms

Bathrooms seem to be the perfect environment for plants. All that warmth and water splashing about makes us feel that anything growing there will thrive. Also, from the point of view of appearance, foliage plants, in particular, are most effective. Their leaf shapes and textures produce a strong contrast with the smooth monochrome forms of bathroom fittings.

There are several advantages in keeping lots of greenery in a bathroom, not least because this room in the house is usually empty for much of the day and the plants are out of the way until bath or shower time; then suddenly there is a fog of hot steam and clouds of talcum powder not to mention spray-drift from anti-perspirants or perfume.

Many bathrooms these days receive constant gentle heat from a towel rail or radiator and provide a pleasantly equable climate for houseplants. There are still many plant possibilities for totally unheated rooms, provided, however, there is some light. Many flats and apartments have internal bathrooms with no natural light so these rooms would be good places to use artificial plants or flowers. If your bathroom seems to have the right conditions then before buying some plants think carefully where you are going to place them. Foliage looks lovely clustered round a bath edge but it is only practical provided you leave room to get in and out, and your house has no boisterous children. Places to put things are often a problem, but one good solution is to run a narrow shelf along a wall or even right round the room at dado height (about a metre

Many plants will thrive in bathroom conditions. The hanging basket is filled with a grape ivy. A kangaroo vine is growing up a cane from the Edwardian cache-pot. Elsewhere there are ferns and another grape ivy. The mirror reflects the greenery to excellent effect.

above the floor) for keeping plants and bottles or pretty decorative things on. Make the most of mirrors in bathrooms to reflect and double the volume of greenery you've got. Mirror tiles on each side of a window reflect dozens of plants from just a couple on the window-sill. Be careful that sunlight is not reflected directly onto the plants as it will scorch the leaves. A hanging basket with say an asparagus fern hung above and a little in front of a wall-mirror does wonders for the atmosphere.

The choice of plants for a bathroom is quite large and may depend on the amount of space you have, but it is a good chance to grow things which demand high humidity such as ferns, or a combination of humidity and warmth such as anthuriums, calatheas, syngoniums or the sweetheart vine (*Philo-*

dendron scandens). Remember that plants such as this, with large areas of leaf, will need occasional sponging to keep them clean. Ivies do well in colder bathrooms putting up with a fair amount of neglect, as do kalanchoes and aglaonemas, but for the maximum effect something with a lusher and more tropical look is the best if your conditions suit it. Flowering plants by their nature tend to be transitory but given enough light will be happy in a bathroom for a short time. One really big bonus for the bathroom is that the bath is the perfect place to take your plants for a warm spray to clean them, or to soak them in a few centimetres of water when they've dried out. There is no excuse for neglected plants in the bathroom; they should be the happiest in the house.

A beautiful streamlined modern bathroom is perfectly set off by the brilliant fresh green of ferns, reflected in a complete wall mirror.

Kitchens

A light bright kitchen window-sill is the perfect place for a collection of different plants. The kitchen table often gets forgotten but it's a great cheer-up to have a seasonal flowering plant on it in a pretty wicker basket.

A kitchen is one of the first rooms people put their plants, even if there are only one or two throughout the whole house. It is probably the room which gets used for the most amount of time by the largest number of people in any household and often has highly suitable conditions for houseplants and other growing things, such as seedlings, pots of herbs, or bulbs, through the winter. Plants and food seem to complement each other aesthetically and even in the coolness of high-tech glossy kitchens a well-chosen plant can cleverly emphasize the room's practicality and functionalism. At the opposite end of the spectrum a decor derived from warm natural materials and earthy colours also benefits enormously from lots of green foliage, emphasizing the homely feel, while somewhere in the middle of the two extremes, where most kitchens are probably found, plants can enliven or calm and add life and texture.

The big problem for most people owning small modern kitchens is simply finding space to put things, so you need to be cunning in placing plants. A window-sill is fine for flowering plants and, if it is quite sunny, cacti and succulents such as crassulas and kalanchoes will thrive as well as pelargoniums which seem to have just the right kitcheny feel about them. Don't leave your plants on the window-sill on cold winter nights unless the window is double glazed because of the danger of frosting. An advantage in many kitchens is the lack of curtains at windows. Often blinds are more practical and it does mean the window-sill can be filled with plants and they don't get horribly tangled with folds of fabric. If you eat in the kitchen a small pot or two of a flowering plant such as a primula on the table in spring is a real cheer-up at meal-times and less bother and expense than cut flowers. Stand them in a pretty bowl or basket.

The tops of wall units are often left empty and bleak and a good trailing plant stood there softens and breaks the hard lines of the unit. Remember it's usually a few degrees warmer up there than the rest of the room so plants dry out quite rapidly. If you don't think you will be bothered to get a chair and get them down to water then think twice about this as a good place to keep them. Some good plants for this high-up location are ivies, tradescantias, asparagus ferns, *Zebrina pendula*, and the spider plant (*Chlorophytum comosum*).

Hanging baskets look marvellous in a kitchen and leave the maximum amount of work-space free. Other plants which look good and like the warmth and humidity of a kitchen include African violets, anthuriums and the firecracker flower (*Crossandra infundibuliformis*).

This busy, narrow corridor-like kitchen manages to squeeze in a plant wherever possible on shelves and ledges. The plants range from a group of little brightly coloured primroses to a palm on the floor and a long trailing Calathea makoyana.

Bedrooms

Once upon a time, plants were never seen in a bedroom. They were considered unhealthy and kept strictly downstairs. They would most likely have greatly suffered upstairs in rooms more often than not kept unheated. In these days of central heating, bedrooms are usually heated, though kept cooler than the rest of the house and at a fairly even temperature, and there is often plenty of space to show plants off to advantage. Sometimes a bedroom is the only room cool enough in a house to grow cyclamens or azaleas well. Both are plants which like quite cool conditions. Bedrooms are often the prettiest rooms in a house but commonly forgotten when houseplants are bought. A pale-pink or cream colour scheme for example, or an all-white lacy bedroom needs the contrast of bright green foliage to bring it alive. Bedroom furniture often has large very bland areas of plain colour which need the change of texture and pattern that comes from a foliage plant such as *Ficus benjamina* or even from a little plant such as *Pilea cadierei* or *Hypoestes phyllostachya*. For pure luxury and a sense of hedonism a beautifully scented plant such as a hoya or *Jasminum polyanthum*

Fresh green foliage plants are the perfect accompaniment for a creamy-beige colour scheme. Here they form an elegant link between the functional furniture and the frilly bed linen. The straw-coloured lilies blend beautifully with the pale tan of the rattan blinds.

or a pot of lilies, or 'Paperwhite' narcissi in spring, make spectacular bedroom plants.

If you simply need splashes of colour to emphasize a particular scheme, then a hibiscus, begonia or chrysanthemum would make a perfect choice for bedroom conditions. For something more everyday, providing there is enough light, a *Fatsia japonica* is a good choice and will slowly grow quite large. The variegated version of this is very pretty and delicate and would look super in a bedroom. A spare bedroom is a good place to overwinter pelargoniums, fuchsias and other plants such as cacti which might need

a cool period of rest. But even if this room is a rest home for worn out plants they can still be grouped together prettily and an eye can be kept on them so they don't turn into a dust-laden dried-out mess.

If you don't want a large plant or group of plants in a bedroom, a small basket with two or three variegated ivies together or the cold-hardy piggy-back plant (*Tolmiea menziesii*) with its soft, pale-green foliage would look lovely on a dressing table or bedside table, especially in a spare bedroom, which is not heated at all times and therefore colder than the rest of the house.

A town bedroom decorated in a very pretty and feminine way needs plants to set it off. This room has plenty of light and therefore many different varieties can be grown. There is a good mix of large floor-standing plants and smaller delicate flowering and foliage plants.

Porches and Conservatories

Porches come in all shapes and sizes and can be tacked on to any side of a house so the amount of sun they receive can vary enormously. Most usually do have lots of light but they are cold and often draughty. A conservatory or glazed addition to a house is a different matter as they are usually heated and insulated even if only to keep temperatures above freezing on winter nights, but a porch, built to protect a main door, isn't thought of as a room in its own right and is often not heated.

It is a really rewarding place to have plants as they give such a lovely warm welcome to visitors and there are surprisingly quite a few plants which are perfectly happy in these rather Spartan conditions. A porch which is simply a shelter from the weather but is still open to the air will only be suitable for the kinds of hardy outdoor plants which you might grow in tubs in the garden: a bay tree perhaps or something with scented foliage

A light sunny porch can be used for lots of seasonal plants. Tubs and pots planted with flowering pelargoniums make a lovely welcoming effect. They will provide colour for several months of the year and can be moved right outside during the warmest periods.

such as lemon verbena (*Lippia citriodora*) which releases its beautiful scent when you brush past it or pinch a leaf. If the light is not very strong then plants should be allowed to bask outside every now and again.

A more closed-in and protected, but cold, porch is a good place for a collection of cacti which can stand low temperatures with little harm. You could instead decide to concentrate on summer plants in your porch and make a spectacular display during the warmer months of the year. There are dozens of annuals which could be potted-up such as morning glory (*Ipomoea violacea*), the pretty yellow Canary creeper nasturtium (*Tropaeolum peregrinum*), black-eyed Susan (*Thunbergia alata*), or the wonderfully scented half-hardy tobacco plant *Nicotiana alata*. This is a tall plant with large white fragrant flowers. The tiny-leaved foliage plant, helxine or mind your own business (*Helxine soleirolii*), once beloved by cottagers, comes in three types, plain green, silver variegated and golden and looks effective in a mass or simply in a low row. Saxifrages, pelargoniums, fuchsias and jasmine in the same way as soleirolia, are happy with cool conditions and shade, and would be ideal if your porch only gets strong light for part of the day. In spring, primulas and cinerarias would thrive in these conditions and later hydrangeas could take over to give plenty of colour throughout the summer. If you have plenty of space a plant of the pale-blue-flowered *Plumbago capensis* would look spectacular and although it's very vigorous it can be cut hard back after flowering to keep it in bounds. It does like plenty of light so is perfect for a glass porch.

If you are lucky enough to own a conservatory, and more and more people are building them as a sensible way to create more space and make a perfect plant-growing environment, then all kinds of opportunities for keeping exciting plants open up. A conservatory provides plenty of light and if kept slightly heated many plants which wouldn't be happy indoors because of the dry atmosphere and low light levels can be successfully grown. The whole subject is vast and there are plenty of books covering this specialized area of indoor gardening.

A beautifully cared for conservatory planted with a great mixture of plants including ferns, hydrangea, asparagus ferns, a vine and palms. With the addition of some artificial heat a huge range of plants can be grown.

This hall has the advantage of a variety of light sources and lots of places to stand plants. A very tall variegated ivy trained to a cane makes a bold effect against the foreground wall. Groups of smaller plants such as Dieffenbachia and mother-in-law's tongue add interest at floor level.

Halls

The biggest problems in an average hall are lack of light and draught. Front doors are sometimes glazed but if not walls often rely on light coming through doorways from other rooms or perhaps from a landing window. If you have a larger than normal hall, and some can be as big as an average room, then you really do need some green plants to cheer up what can be a very gloomy empty space. Draughts can cause difficulties too and, obviously, plants need to be chosen which won't be damaged or get in the way in what is quite a busy thoroughfare in any house.

There are some plants which will put up with these conditions such as aglaonema or the even tougher aspidistra. But to be more positive, many people have lovely light warm halls with no problem at all where they can grow all manner of different plants. One large plant or a group making a permanent feature may seem a good idea and should be fine if the plants don't get forgotten and they have plenty of care lavished on them. Nothing looks more depressing than a dusty neglected plant, and a hall is the place where first impressions are made. Perhaps it is best to think of any plant arrangement as being temporary and then you can change things around often and use plants which wouldn't be happy in the situation for long periods of time. A basis of green plants plus one flowering plant would look good. Two handsome foliage plants a monstera and a ×*Fatshedera lizei*, or perhaps a kentia palm or a spathiphyllum would be suitable where you need strong positive shapes, and for small groupings on a table or shelf some of the *Maranta* species have very pretty leaf markings and prefer a shady position in the house. Ivies are another tough and easy plant for a hall and a large bowl with three or more small-leaved types put together and allowed to flop gently downwards instead of stiffly fixed to canes is an easy and effective option. At night time spotlighting can do wonders in halls to highlight a plant and brighten a dark corner. A piece of furniture such as a chest or side table would look splendid with a seasonal pot of flowering bulbs in spring, a Christmassy poinsettia or a begonia in brilliant flower during the spring or summer.

This enormous yucca strangely echoes the form of the spiral staircase. In a position such as this, on a busy landing, a plant that needs little attention but always looks good is the best choice.

Large Windows

An enormous window space such as this at the top of a conservatory makes it possible to grow dozens of plants. The clever use of hanging baskets allows the maximum amount of space to be filled. The tall Ficus benjamina standing in front relates the window to the rest of the room.

Large areas of glass in the house are a relatively modern phenomenon and perhaps it is not surprising that since we have been letting more light into our houses we have been growing more plants as well. Houses these days are warmer and lighter than ever before and the plant breeders manage to keep us supplied with more and more new types to take full advantage of this. In the last decade thousands of houses have had patio doors installed in living rooms, adding light, sunshine and a new view all at once. Aesthetically, plants grouped near a large window soften the break between indoors and outdoors so that the interior blends with the garden. Glass down to the floor obviously means that window-sills have been done away with and new homes have to be found for smaller plants. Tall plants can be stood on the ground a little way back from the glass or hanging plants can frame the sides and top of a huge expanse of glass. Big double-glazed windows obviously eliminate cold wintry draughts but if they face south they can also create scorching summer conditions when the sun is at its strongest. Many plants cannot survive

powerful direct sunlight so plant arrangements must be flexible to cope with this where it is going to be a problem. Rattan blinds or fine narrow Venetian blinds may even be necessary for a room which simply gets too hot in the summer. Any plant growing near a light source will lean towards it and so needs turning regularly to avoid a lop-sided lean and lanky look.

A large area of glass demands something splendid in size – a small tree or tall palm to make bold shapes and outlines against the window. Large windows which do not reach to the floor and have a window-sill provide a

very good home for lots of houseplants such as the light-loving croton family, but always take care that the leaves are not actually touching the glass, especially during cold winter nights or in strong direct sunlight. A shelf fitted above a radiator to deflect heat away from plants is a good idea if your heat source is under a window, as it so often is. The area near a big bay window or patio doors will probably be the best place in the house to grow many types of plants so it is worth experimenting with things until you've created a display which you like and which satisfactorily meets your needs.

This specially designed frame displaying a collection of cacti is based on window shapes and hangs well in front of the real window. Cacti are tough and will stand the extreme conditions experienced near a window – strong sun and heat as well as cold and draughts.

Dry Atmosphere

Studies and workrooms are often dry and dark but benefit enormously from the addition of some colourful plants. In impossible places the best choice is artificial plants, which now come in dozens of different varieties. **Right** *Fuchsia, fern and African violets have been arranged to disguise a radiator.* **Below** *Yellow primulas and a chrysanthemum brighten a study corner.*

However hard you try some rooms just don't suit houseplants. They are either too dark, and no plants can do without light, or they are too warm and this is a problem when it goes hand in hand with low humidity. Some of the problem can be eliminated by using electric humidifiers or the water-filled variety that is attached to a radiator. Grouping plants together improves their chances of prospering and maturing. Also standing the pots on a base of pebbles or plunging into peat, which is then kept damp, helps immensely. Alternatively you can give up the struggle with the fine mist sprayer and grow plants which naturally come from arid regions of the world. This doesn't mean that they never have to be watered, although most cacti and succulents can be left for quite long periods without attention. However, many people once they've started collecting plants of this type become very enthusiastic about the whole `thing and growing them becomes a major hobby. There are specialist nurseries supplying fabulously rare and exotic types, but any that are commonly available are probably easy to cultivate. Some cacti shapes are exciting or even weird and often look their best in cool modern surroundings.

If you have a room such as a study or spare bedroom with little natural light which simply does not give plants a chance then some other kind of decoration will have to be used. Artificial plants and flowers have come a very long way since dusty plastic

daffodils and there is now a marvellous range of fabric flowers and dried real flowers to choose from. Newest of all are the artificial plants which are wonderfully accurate in colour and texture and demand nothing more than the occasional dusting. There are dozens to choose from including foliage plants such as ferns and colourful flowering plants such as cyclamen and chrysanthemums. You can either choose to pretend they are real and use them in positions where you might have the real versions, or put them in unlikely places and show off that they are frankly fake.

If you don't like the idea of one material pretending to be another then dried flowers are for you. There is a fantastic choice available now and many florists sell bunches of dried flowers as well as ready-made arrangements. To be at their most effective they should be used generously not spikily and sparsely. If you don't have the confidence to arrange flowers yourself then buy several bunches of one type of flower in a single colour and arrange them in a pretty container. This is far more stunning than mixing colours and shapes and getting it wrong. Artificial plants and flowers and dried natural flowers are wonderful for rooms which are too dark or too dry for the real thing or for rooms used infrequently, or in the winter when many houses are too dark for really successful plant growing.

Begonia masoniana

Begonia masoniana
Iron cross begonia
Height: 20-25cm (8-10in)
Spread: 25-30cm (10-12in)
Minimum winter temperature:
13°C (55°F).
Well-known large-leaved tuberous evergreen and long-lived begonia, with mid-green, corrugated, hairy leaves with four or five bronze-purple cross-like bars radiating from the centres. It seldom flowers. *Begonia rex* is also tuberous and large-leaved, with forms in a wide range of colours and patterns.
They all require a well-lit position but out of direct sunlight, with large plants being re-potted in April. Do not overwater.

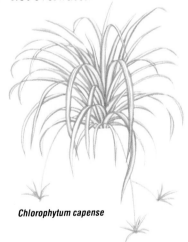

Chlorophytum capense

Chlorophytum capense
also sold as
Chlorophytum elatum
Spider plant
St. Bernard's lily
Height: 20-25cm (8-10in)
Spread: 38-60cm (15-24in)
Minimum winter temperature:
7°C (45°F)

A familiar foliage houseplant with a sprawling nature, created by the long, narrow, arching, mid-green leaves with narrow white strips down their centres. Botanists are not in harmony about the naming of this plant and its near relatives, and often it is *Chloropytum comosum* 'Variegatum' that is offered for sale, displaying long, narrow mid-green leaves edged white. It also produces long, spider-like stems with small plants at their ends. These can be pegged down into pots of compost to develop roots. John Innes potting compost or a peat-based type are suitable. Make sure the compost does not become dry.

Chrysanthemum
Height: 15-25cm (6-10in)
Spread: 20-30cm (8-12in)
Minimum winter temperature:
7°C (45°F).
Chrysanthemums that were once sold in their millions as cut-flowers during autumn and early winter are now often grown the year-round as pot plants. By carefully controlling the length of light during a twenty-four hour period they can now be made to flower at any time of the year. Chemicals are often used to ensure the plants remain small and compact, therefore it is not worth trying to grow the plants on for a second year; discard them after flowering. Chrysanthemums are best bought in bud, with colour just showing. Do not let the compost dry out as there is usually a large number of plants in one pot and they quickly flag when dry. As long-life and reliable flowering houseplants in the home they have few equals.

Cyclamen persicum
Alpine violet
Height: 15-23cm (6-9in)
Spread: 15-25cm (6-10in)
Minimum winter temperature:
7-10°C (45-50°F).

From this species are derived well-known winter-flowering houseplants sold in millions at Christmas. They need little description, the dainty, scented, butterfly-like flowers standing above the dark-green, prettily silver-marbled leaves. Flower colour ranges from white to red.
The plants are best bought when in bud and just showing colour, and will require a cool, draught-free spot with a constant temperature. Take care to keep the compost just moist, without it becoming over-saturated.

× Fatshedera lizei
Tree ivy or Climbing figleaf
Height: 90cm-1.5m (3-5ft)
Spread: 30-60cm (1-2ft)
Minimum winter temperature:
4°C (37°F)

× *Fatshedera lizei*

Botanically interesting cross between two distinct plants – known as the 'botanical wonder' in America – with leathery, five-lobed, glossy, deep-green leaves. Greenish-white flowers appear on established plants during October and November.
The plant can be trained as a climber, when it exceeds the above height, or cut back several times during its life to give a bushy appearance. Position out of direct sunlight during summer, as it may quickly wilt.

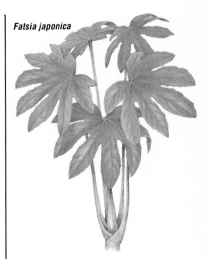

Fatsia japonica

Fatsia japonica
Height: 1.5-1.8m (5-6ft)
Spread: 1.2-1.5m (4-5ft)
Minimum winter temperature:
2°C (36°F).
A fully-hardy slow-growing evergreen shrub. Outdoors it will eventually grow up to 3.5m (12ft) or more high, but is used during its early years as a beautiful houseplant, with rich glossy green, palmate leaves formed of seven to nine coarsely-toothed lobes.
Large specimens do best in John Innes potting compost. Re-pot during spring, at the same time detaching sucker-like growths and potting them separately.

Ficus benjamina

Ficus benjamina
Weeping fig
Height: 1.5-1.8m (5-6ft)
Spread: 90cm-1m (3-3½ft)
Minimum winter temperature:
16-18°C (61-64°F).
Vigorous tree-like evergreen houseplant with upright stems, drooping at their tips,

and slightly pendulous dark green spear-shaped and slender-painted leaves, light green when young.
Both John Innes potting compost and peat-based types are suitable, although the J.I. compost is better for large specimens as it is heavier and produces more stable plants. Cuttings 5-10cm (2-4in) long of lateral shoots can be taken in April and May in 16°C (61°F). Do not over water. Requires bright light in the winter.

Hedera
Ivies
Height: Varies greatly according to situation.
Minimum winter temperature: 2°C (36°F).
These are some of the most widely grown and reliable foliage houseplants, mostly derived from our native *Hedera helix*, the common ivy. The forms used in the home are small-leaved varieties, selected because of their attractive shape and colours. John Innes potting compost or a peat-based type suits them, and they are easily increased from small cuttings, 7.5-13cm (3-5in) long, taken in early summer and inserted to about one-third of their length in equal parts peat and sharp sand.

Helxine soleirolii
Mind your own business
Baby's tears
now correctly
Soleirolia soleirolii
Height: Prostrate
Minimum winter temperature: 4°C (39°F).
An interesting creeping plant, often forming a wide and trailing mat of small, rounded pale to mid-green leaves. Two forms are especially worth growing: *Helxine soleirolii* 'Argentea' with silvery variegated leaves, and *Helxine soleirolii* 'Aurea' with golden-green leaves.
John Innes potting compost suits it well. Split up and

Helxine soleirolii

divide overcrowded plants in spring. Ensure the plants have plenty of water during summer.

Hoya carnosa

Hoya carnosa
Wax flower
Height: 3.5-4.5m (12-15ft), climber
Minimum winter temperature: 10°C (50°F).
Eventually this evergreen climber may exceed the above figure in a greenhouse, but as a small plant it can bring fragrance to a room with its May to September star-shaped white to flesh-pink flowers with 7.5cm (3in) wide heads. Variegated foliage forms are available, one with pink edges to the leaves, the other with yellowish to cream centres and green edges.
Hoya bella, the Miniature wax flower or Shower of stars, is

small and shrubby and grows to only 30cm (1ft) high, displaying May to September waxy white flowers in 5cm (2in) heads.
John Innes potting compost or a peat-based type are suitable.

Hypoestes phyllostachya
Polka dot plant
also sold as
Hypoestes sanguinolenta
Height: 45-60cm (1½-2ft)
Spread: 38-45cm (15-18in)
Minimum winter temperature: 10° (50°F).

Hypoestes phyllostachya

Restful-looking foliage houseplant, with oval, spear-shaped, dark-green leaves covered with pink blotches or dots. However, the colouring varies in intensity from one plant to another. If left the plant often achieves 60cm (2ft) in height, but by repeatedly nipping out the growing tips from the young plant a sprawling habit can be achieved.
It does best in slight shade.

Kalanchoe blossfeldiana
Height: 20-30cm (8-12in)
Spread: 15-25cm (6-10in)
Minimum winter temperature: 7°C (45°F).
Widely grown erect, bushy succulent houseplant that can be made to flower at any time of the year by giving the plants 'short-day' treatment to

initiate bud development. Normally, flowering is from February to May. The broad, scalloped-edged, ovate, mid-green leaves are fleshy. The scarlet flowers are borne in dense heads above them. Many forms are available; *Kalanchoe blossfeldiana* 'Vulcan' is sturdy and dwarf, with bright scarlet flowers.
John Innes composts are suitable. Re-pot in spring. It survives well on window-sills.

Nicotiana alata
Tobacco plant
also known as
Nicotiana affinis
Height: 60-75cm (2-2½ft)
Spread: 20-25cm (8-10in)
Minimum temperature: 5°C (41°F).
A half-hardy perennial usually grown as a half-hardy annual to flower in an open border, but can be sown earlier under glass in a temperature of 18°C (64°F) to produce plants to flower under glass or in the home. After the plants are established the temperature can be reduced. The plants are well-known, with oblong mid-green leaves and white, tubular, highly-scented flowers, 7.5cm (3in) long, from May onwards.
John Innes potting compost suits it, but ensure that it does not dry out. Slight shade is appreciated.

Pellaea rotundifolia

Pellaea rotundifolia
Button fern
Height: 15-23cm (6-9in)
Spread: 25-30cm (10-12in)
Minimum winter temperature: 7°C (45°F).

Distinctive small, easily grown fern with wiry stems bearing about twenty small, button-like, leathery leaves, dark green above and light green beneath. Give it an open, well-drained compost and position away from direct sunlight. Keep it out of draughts.

Philodendron scandens
Sweetheart vine
Height: 1.2-1.8m (4-6ft), climber
Minimum winter temperature: 8°C (46°F) but for limited periods only.

Philodendron scandens

Beautiful easily grown climber with plain green, somewhat heart-shaped and pointed leaves. A variegated form is available with cream-blotched leaves.
Peat-based composts suit it well. Keep them well-watered during summer and just moist the rest of the year. Position in good light, but not in direct sun.

Plumbago capensis
Cape leadwort
also sold as
Plumbago auriculata
Height: 3m (10ft), climber
Minimum winter temperature: 7°C (45°F).

An evergreen flowering, climbing houseplant with mid-green leaves and 25-30cm (10-12in) long clusters of phlox-like, pale blue flowers, 2.5cm (1in) wide, from spring to late autumn.

Plumbago capensis

John Innes potting compost suits it well. Keep the compost well moist during flowering. Re-pot in spring.

Setcreasea pallida
often sold as
Setcreasea purpurea
Height: 30-38cm (12-15in)
Spread: 38-45cm (15-18in)
Minimum winter temperature: 7°C (45°F).

Setcreasea pallida

Straggly, spreading foliage houseplant with upright tufts of narrow lance-shaped slightly hairy purple leaves. From early summer to late autumn it bears clusters of three-petalled purplish flowers.
John Innes potting composts or a peat-based type are suitable. The richest leaf colours are encouraged by setting the plants in good light but not in direct and strong sunlight.

Tolmiea menziesii
Piggy-back plant
Pig-a-back plant
Youth-on-age
Thousand mothers
Height: 13-15cm (5-6in)
Spread: 20-25cm (8-10in)
Minimum winter temperature: full hardy plant if acclimatized in summer.

A delightfully reliable clump-forming foliage houseplant, ideal for cold rooms and porches, with pale green and slightly hairy maple-like leaves. During June it displays erect stems, up to 45cm (1½ft) high, with greenish-white tubular flowers.
John Innes potting compost suits it well. Take care not to water it excessively during the winter.

Tradescantia albiflora
Wandering jew
Height: Trailing
Minimum winter temperature: 7°C (45°F).

Well-known somewhat straggly foliage houseplant, ideal in a hanging-basket or as a trailer over the side of a shelf. It has

Tradescantia albiflora

oval, stemless green leaves; however, it is invariably the forms with variegated leaves that are grown, such as *Tradescantia albiflora* 'Tricolor' with rose-purple and white stripes.
Tradescantia fluminensis is similar, with slightly longer oval leaves borne on short leaf stalks. The most popular form is 'Quicksilver'.
John Innes potting composts or a peat-based type suit them well. Situate in a well-lit spot but out of direct sun. Pinch back frequently to encourage bushy growth.

Zebrina pendula

Zebrina pendula
Inch plant
Height: Trailing
Minimum winter temperature: 7°C (45°F).

Sprawling, somewhat straggly foliage houseplant – often confused with tradescantias – with oval leaves displaying two lustrous silvery bands on either side of a mid-green background. The leaves are purple beneath. From June to September it displays three-petalled purple flowers.
The form *Zebrina pendula* 'Quadricolor' displays white and purple striped leaves.
John Innes potting composts or peat-based types suit it well. It prefers a well-lit position out of direct sun.

NOOKS & CRANNIES

Although for much of the time we choose a houseplant because we like the look of it, we sometimes pick one to fill a special position, where we know from experience it will be highly successful. As well as the obvious places there are dozens of other less obvious ones throughout the house which, with a little thought, can be transformed by the right choice of plant. Most houses have alcoves and recesses, dull corners or redundant fireplaces, all of which could do with being brightened up and put to good use. Even the most unlikely spaces can make a home for some kind of plant. Here are ideas for plants to fit any odd empty corner you might have.

A fireplace in summer needs some adornment and here a simple mixture of asparagus fern and brilliant scarlet begonia does the job perfectly.

Fireplaces

This warm, cream and apricot interior benefits enormously from all the fresh green foliage. The fireplace otherwise would look quite blank.

A fireplace is a warming and cheerful thing in winter if you have a coal or wood fire burning, or even if it is occupied by an electric or gas heater. Summertime is a different matter as all there is to look at is a rather dusty and depressing black hole. Bedroom fireplaces, uncovered perhaps after years of being blocked up, are very rarely used for their original purpose but rather as a decorative feature of the room, and often they are so pretty they definitely ought to be shown off. A fireplace by its shape is a natural frame or surround for whatever fills the space inside so this is a chance to use plants creatively and stylishly, knowing they will be set off beautifully. A summer hearth is fun to fill with flowers, dried ones if you want to do it just once for the whole season, or plants, either foliage ones or the flowering kind. It doesn't usually matter if the odd drop of water is spilt on a hearth, and the grate works like a basket, containing the whole display. Even a solid-fuel stove bene-fits from a plant stood on it in summer as a redundant heater looks just as sad as an

Cissus rhombifolia *on the left,* Philodendron scandens *in the centre and Cissus* antarctica *on the right are three foliage plants which can happily spend the summer months in a redundant fireplace.*

empty hearth and people still tend to focus on the fireplace even on summer evenings.

Ferns are often chosen to fill an empty fireplace and their form, with leaves spilling out from the centre, is particularly suited to the angle which they will be seen from. The leaf outline is especially attractive, thrown into relief by a dark surround. Bedroom fireplaces are excellent for ferns as they tend to be cooler rooms than those downstairs and ferns are happy in fairly shady surroundings, though they do need an atmosphere which is not too dry. Choose other foliage plants which have good leaf shapes and any with strong markings or colours. A muddle of thin and spiky leaves will not be very effective but the glossy foliage and definite outline of a fatsia or schefflera would have just the right effect, or try the beautifully cream-splashed leaves of *Ctenanthe oppenheimiana tricolor* which is happy in shady conditions.

Flowering plants will also look good in an empty fireplace but if their own foliage is not very impressive they may need another green plant to keep them company.

Hallways

The problems of growing and keeping plants in hallways has been discussed on p.56. It can be a difficult area in the house but also very rewarding if you manage to assemble a good plant display. If there is no space for a large floor-standing plant then there is usually a piece of furniture, perhaps a table or chest or even a shelf, on which to stand a small plant or arrangement. A little group of several small plants can look very pretty, mixing a few foliage plants with a flowering one and showing the complete thing off in a basket or shallow cache-pot. A pretty mixture might be a small-leaved variegated ivy,

an African violet, choosing from the wide range of colours available now, including white, and a small-leaved plant such as a fern or pilea. If you want one magnificent plant to make a really strong impact then choose with care to suit your particular surroundings. If the hall is quite light then there is a wide range to choose from; if it is dark and gloomy then the choice is rather limited. *Monstera deliciosa* is often seen used in entrance halls and if it is grown well can look superb, but it does have a rather unfriendly and institutional look about it in a house because we are so used to seeing it in public buildings and offices and it does

A well thought-out group of foliage plants stands at the end of a hallway. All are species of ficus but very different in style. Ficus elastica is on the left, Ficus radicans is in the centre with Ficus pumila above it, and on the right is Ficus benjamina.

have a tendency to become leggy. Better by far to grow a few less-clichéd plants and make a group with perhaps *Philodendron Laciniatum* (*P. pedatum*) in the background. It will happily fill a lofty corner given time.

Plants in the palm family really need space and air surrounding them visually; they need to be seen in the round and not cluttered by furniture and walls, so most halls would not provide the best position to show them off to advantage. A great spacious black and white chequered tiled hall, however, would look magnificent with one or two palms standing on the floor or on plant stands that suit the period of architecture. Where there is a staircase with a bend, there

is often space for a group of plants. For safety's sake keep the arrangement quite small and fix the containers to the wall if necessary. Any tall plant standing in a hall needs a large solid container to keep the whole thing safe and stable. Smaller plants could be grouped in a display stand of some kind, perhaps made from cane or willow. These are usually fairly narrow and would stand against a wall in a hall quite successfully. Antique and old wire plant stands can still be found. Usually painted white or green, they were once used in conservatories but make perfect homes for plants where you want a decorative display to be viewed from one side.

This hallway has a large window which provides really good conditions for a collection of foliage plants. Tucked away on a ledge out of any danger of being a nuisance, they can flourish and create a green screen.

A dark and dull corner is brought to life by the over-sized glossy leaves of a Monstera deliciosa. *As long as this plant is well cared for and the leaves are kept clean and shiny it can be relied on to provide impact.*

Dull Corners

Every room however carefully planned usually ends up with a dull corner or two. Most furniture has straight sides and squarish shapes and simply doesn't fill corners perfectly so empty gaps happen whether we like it or not. Low seating units are often placed at right angles to each other with a coffee table put where the two meet. Behind it there is an inevitable blank. Pictures and prints are generally hung on walls in central positions so that they can be seen at their best leaving the corners bare. A corner by its nature may only receive a small amount of

light but in a room with a good source of natural light to start with there should be enough to grow quite a few types of plant.

The choice of how to display a plant or group of plants in a corner is wide. You could use a hanging basket fixed either from the ceiling or from a wall bracket, a specially made corner shelf unit or a container standing on the floor for a tall plant. Small plants can be placed on a low piece of furniture or plant stand. One of the prettiest shapes of plant to grow in a corner is the standard form, that is a tall bare stem with all the growth branching out from the top.

Yuccas are often treated in this way. They are cut off at a height upwards of a metre and allowed to regrow from the top of the stem. Fuchsias are very pretty made into standard trees as their growth is naturally weeping and very graceful. *Ficus benjamina* can often be grown as a small tree. You can also devise your own tree shapes by putting a bushy fern such as *Nephrolepis exaltata* or the soft and delicate *Asparagus sprengeri* on a slender plant stand where it will cascade down.

Of course not all corners are large; there are dozens of little places which simply look bare and need cheering up. Again anywhere that is really dark will make a plant suffer so it may be best to fill it with artificial or dried flowers and not attempt to grow anything. Good plants for temporarily brightening up the gloom are pots of brilliant jewel-coloured primroses; they get very straggly in fact if given too much bright light indoors. Pots of begonias really shine out with their strong colours and a group of good-natured kalanchoes, which are now available in a variety of colours, would liven up any dull shelf end or forgotten corner.

There is often a gap left where one piece of furniture meets another at right angles. Standing a plant in the gap, perhaps on a low table, is an ideal way of using the space. Fatsia japonica has beautiful foliage and an elegant growing habit and ideally fills the gap

Alcoves

Alcoves and recesses may be either planned and constructed when a house is built or incorporated later when alterations are made, for instance, when a staircase is moved or a chimney-breast changed. They are ideal spots for displaying a collection of glass or any other small attractive objects you wish to focus attention on. In a hall, where the space under the stairs has been left open, or in an open-plan room where the stairs themselves may be open there is plenty of scope for exciting arrangements of plants, particularly hanging and trailing ones.

Occasionally old houses have many odd little alcoves and recesses and it's impossible to know how best to use them. Plants can do wonders here but in some cases may need the help of extra light to keep them well and to maximise their visual effect. A well-proportioned alcove makes a perfect backdrop for a special plant but whatever you choose has to be good enough to stand the extra notice it will get. This may be the place to concentrate on a magnificent flowering plant of some kind. Choose from the huge range available now according to the time of year. A *Hydrangea macrophylla* or a *Hibiscus rosa-sinensis* would make a splendid feature and in the winter months cyclamen or azaleas could take over. The brilliant red bracts of poinsettia or the more subtle greeny-white or coral versions make a perfect Christmas arrangement.

If you want a more permanent plant for an alcove or recess then choose something which has good leaf shape or particularly pretty or unusual leaf markings. A position like this will throw the plant into relief and it needs lots of character as its greenery will be its chief feature. *Maranta leuconeura erythroneura* (prayer plant) has wonderfully marked leaves and is happy out of strong sunlight, and caladiums, though not the easiest plants to cultivate, have the most exquisite leaf colours and patterns which need a background to throw them into focus. Plants suitable for under a staircase are limited but if you have space on an open-tread stair and no small children to kick or pull plants down then all kinds of hanging plants could be stood on the stairs, or it might be possible to fasten them to the banister rails and grow small trailing ivies or spider plants.

These shelf units look attractive filled with foliage and they are deep enough to take good-sized plants. It's as well to turn plants regularly in these positions so they don't grow all in one direction.

A splendid but rather forbidding stove and mantelpiece has a happy mix of plants echoing the green from the glossy tile surround. In this case the plain black plant pots have exactly the right feel to them and don't need covering up.

Mantelpieces

Mantelpieces come in all shapes and sizes, tall and low, wide or shallow and may be made from quite different materials, stone, wood or ceramic. The problems they present as homes for plants are their very limited size, at least in terms of depth from front to back, and the warmth rising from a fire. Often this is not as severe as you might think. They are usually a good distance away from the real heat source and the ledge tends to deflect the heat out into the room, not up to the ceiling. The fireplace is a focus in any room even if it is not being used and the mantelpiece is often used to display treasured possessions. A carefully chosen plant or two can add enormously to the complete arrangement. Very often things on a mantelpiece are arranged symmetrically: a clock in the centre flanked by two matching candlesticks or ceramics. Complete the picture with two matching plants or alternatively produce a focus of attention by carefully positioning one plant.

Choose containers which blend with the colour scheme or use them to make a strong contrast in colour terms. You have the choice of stiff upright plants, small mounds of soft foliage or a trailing type of plant to break the straight horizontal lines of the mantelpiece. This is one place in the house where a plant will be closely looked at and is therefore an ideal opportunity to use some of the intricate and small-leaved varieties which need to be peered at to appreciate their form and texture. A mantelpiece is also a marvellous place to stand a special pot of flowering bulbs for their brief and lovely life. Very often they are scented and need to be easily accessible to be fully appreciated. A small pot of crocus or Iris reticulata bring a tiny patch of brilliant colour to dull wintry days. If your mantelpiece is bare and uncluttered by anything then you could fill its whole length with plants. You could begin by putting a tallish plant in the centre and standing progressively smaller plants towards the edges creating a pyramid of foliage. Vary the textures and colours of foliage types and, if you use flowering kinds as well, the arrangements will be more effective if only the shades of one colour are used. This idea would be lovely for a special occasion.

Aglaonema commutatum
Chinese evergreen
Height: 15cm (6in)
Spread: 23-30cm (9-12in)
Minimum winter temperature:
10°C (50°F).

An evergreen perennial houseplant with dark-green lance-shaped leaves, dappled greyish-silver, and white arum-like flowers during July. The form *Aglaonema commutatum* 'Treubii' (often sold as *Aglaonema treubii*) has red berries and is smaller and more compact. *Aglaonema crispum* 'Silver Queen' displays silvery variegation in its leaves.

Aglaonema commutatum

John Innes potting compost or a peat-based type are suitable. Keep away from draughty and chilly positions.

Asparagus sprengeri
sometimes sold under
Asparagus densiflorus
'Sprengeri'
Asparagus fern
Height: 30-38cm (12-15in)
Spread: 90cm-1m (3-3½ft)
Minimum winter temperature:
7°C (45°F).

Superb hanging-basket evergreen foliage plant with wiry, arching stems loosely clustered with stiff, narrow, mid-green leaves that give the plant a fern-like appearance – although it is not a true fern. The form *Asparagus sprengeri* 'Compactus', with compact and erect growth, is better as a pot plant.
John Innes potting compost suits it well. Take care not to

Asparagus sprengeri

water it excessively during winter. Position out of direct light during summer.

Caladium × hortulanum
Angel's wings
Height: 23-38cm (9-15in)
Spread: 25-30cm (10-12in)
Minimum winter temperature:
15°C (59°F).

Caladium × hortulanum

Attractively leaved foliage houseplant. It is very difficult to grow from tubers yourself, as it needs a temperature of 21°C (71°F) as well as high humidity to start into growth. Most people, therefore, buy established plants in late spring and early summer. The wide, arrowhead-shaped leaves are borne on long stems and are plain and

uninteresting at first; later they develop white, cream or red markings. There are many named varieties.
It is a plant that suffers when given fluctuating temperatures, a draughty position or direct sunlight.

Cocos weddeliana

Cocos weddeliana
now correctly known as
Syagrus weddeliana
Height: 1.2-1.8m (4-6ft)
Spread: 90cm-1.5m (3-5ft)
Minimum winter temperature:
16°C (61°F).

A slow-growing, wide-spreading palm, ideal for a palm stand, with narrow, delicate, dark-green fronds. Although in favourable conditions it can reach the height given above, it seldom exceeds 45cm (1½ft). John Innes potting compost suits it well, but keep it moist during summer. Re-pot during spring, every two or three years. Likes high humidity.

Crocus chrysanthus
Height: 7.5-10cm (3-4in)
Spread: 2.5-4cm (1-1½in)
Minimum winter temperature:
5-7°C (41-45°F).
These small-flowered irises are a must for mid-winter and early-spring flowering indoors in a cool room.
Characteristically the species displays delightful golden-

yellow flowers, but there are now many varieties to choose from, in a wide colour range, sometimes flecked or streaked. They can be bought in pots ready for flowering, or planted seven or eight to a 15cm (6in) pot of John Innes potting compost in autumn as soon as the corms are available. They should be given cool conditions and brought into a cool room when the shoots appear.

Ctenanthe oppenheimiana
tricolor
Height: 15-23cm (6-9in)
Spread: 25-38cm (10-15in)
Minimum winter temperature:
16°C (61°F).
Beautiful foliage houseplant with a sprawling and spreading but dense nature. It has long, spear-shaped leaves boldly marked with light and dark green, as well as cream and fawn. Contrastingly, the undersides are purple.

Ctenanthe oppenheimiana

John Innes potting compost suits it well. Ensure that it does not dry out. Strong sunlight during summer, draughts and temperature fluctuations can cause the leaves to brown at their edges or the colours to fade.

Euphorbia pulcherrima
Poinsettia
Height: 90cm-1.2m (3-4ft)
Spread: 38cm (15in)
Minimum winter temperature:
13-16°C (55-61°F).

Euphorbia pulcherrima

Well-known flowering, deciduous shrub grown for Christmas decoration. Its true flowers are insignificant, and it is the showy leaf-like dazzling red bracts that create colour and interest from November to February. There are also pink, white and cream bract forms. The bright-green leaves are shallowly lobed.

It is usually increased annually from cuttings taken during April and May, but a high temperature is required to induce them to produce roots. When in flower keep the plants away from draughts and do not let the compost become dry.

Hibiscus rosa-sinensis

Hibiscus rosa-sinensis
Chinese rose
Height: 1.5-1.8m (5-6ft)
Spread: 1.2-1.8m (4-6ft)
Minimum winter temperature: 7°C (45°F).

A beautiful tender evergreen shrub, best suited to a large greenhouse but can be grown in 13-15cm (5-6in) pots in the home where it can be kept small and bushy. From early summer to early autumn the plants are covered with large, showy flowers, with projecting clusters of yellow stamens. Several varieties are available, in yellow, salmon, pink and shades of red. For the home *Hibiscus rosa-sinensis* 'Cooperi' is one of the best, being slow-growing and dwarf.

John Innes potting compost or a peat-based type suit it well. Keep the compost moist when the plants are in flower.

Maranta leuconeura

Maranta leuconeura
Prayer plant
Rabbit-track plant
Domino plant
Height: 15-20cm (6-8in)
Spread: 30-38cm (12-15in)
Minimum winter temperature: 13°C (55°F).

These widely sold foliage houseplants are well-known for folding their leaves upright during evening, as if in prayer. Their oval, pointed-tipped and slightly ribbed leaves are bright green at first with brown-purple blotches between the veins.

John Innes potting compost or a peat-based type suit it well. Shade plants from direct sunlight during summer, and divide and re-pot crowded plants in spring.

Monstera deliciosa

Monstera deliciosa
Swiss cheese plant
Height: 1.8m+ (6ft+)
Spread: 1.5m+ (5ft+)
Minimum winter temperature: 10°C (50°F).

Eventually this species becomes a very large foliage houseplant. It is often seen in offices and public buildings, and does best in centrally heated homes where it can be kept growing the year through. The large roundish-oval, shiny, deep green leaves become deeply incised and eventually holes form in mature leaves. Leaves up to 1m (3½ft) long are frequently produced on older well-grown plants. Mature plants develop creamy-yellow arum-like flowers in clusters of two or three, followed by green-white pineapple-like fruits that taste like a combination of banana and pineapple. It is from these that the plant derives part of its name, deliciosa. But beware – these fruits contain sharp fibres.

A John Innes compost will give it a firm base. Water well in the summer and keep the leaves shiny and dust free.

Pilea cadierei
Aluminium plant
Height: 25-30cm (10-12in)
Spread: 25-30cm (10-12in)
Minimum winter temperature: 10°C (50°F).

Distinctive foliage houseplant with narrow, oval, somewhat spear-shaped dark-green leaves, 5-6.5cm (2-2½in) long and with irregular glossy, silvery blotches between the veins. It is usually seen in the form *Pilea cadierei* 'Nana', which is slightly more compact.

Pilea cadierei

John Innes potting compost or a peat-based type are suitable, with water given freely during summer.

Rhododendron simsii
Indian azalea
Height: 25-30cm (10-12in)
Spread: 30-38cm (12-15in)
Minimum winter temperature: 10°C (50°F).

A half-hardy evergreen azalea 'forced' by nurserymen to flower at Christmas and on into early spring. Colour range includes red, pink and white, and the plants are best bought when in bud and just showing colour.

Peaty and fibrous lime-free compost is essential. Keep the compost moist and slowly acclimatize the plants to the above temperature. After flowering place in a cool, frost-free position; place outside during summer.

COLOUR HIGHLIGHTS

Colour is profoundly important in our lives and nowhere more so than in the houses we live in. Very often the first choice made about a room is what colour it should be. Colour can be used to our advantage to create a mood, highlight something special or even trick the eye. Houseplants will do all this, used either on their own or in a subtle mix with fabrics, paint, carpets and furniture. Nowadays there are hundreds of plants to choose from, and more and more flowering types are appearing in a vast range of colours. It is therefore important to consider the whole subject of colour in some detail to get the best from your plants and maybe take a fresh look at how you use them in your home.

Flowering plants can blend with the colours used in a room, as the pale pink azalea does here, or they can add contrasting sparkle and highlights.

Pinks and Reds

Right A bathroom with lots of pink manages not to be sugary by using a strong fabric design and a deep, dull rose pink for the ceramic ware. The cyclamen on the narrow shelf brings the whole scheme alive.

Although pastel colours are now very fashionable, pale powder pink is not the most popular colour for living rooms. Many people, however, choose soft coral, peach or terracotta as the basis for furnishings as it is a welcoming and warm colour and very easy to live with. It can look very rich on its own or quite restrained when mixed with cooler greys, blues or greens. The deepest plummiest reds and rusts definitely need the relief of plenty of green to emphasize their qualities while paler, peachier pinks look marvellous with soft grey greens. There are plenty of flowering plants in this colour range that can be used to emphasize the tints of furnishings or to strengthen pale tones on walls or floors. A few foliage plants also have strong pink or red colouration which is useful when you need a longer life than a flowering plant might provide. There is a great range of flowering plants to choose from here; cineraria, primula, cyclamen and azaleas all come in pinks and reds. Hydrangeas have such large flower heads that

they can add great splashes of pink to a room, and there are plenty of small-flowered plants such as *Catharanthus roseus* or African violets as well as the beautiful pink-leaved caladiums and *Hypoestes sanguinolenta*. Fuchsias come in many varieties nearly all a mix of pink and red and white. Pelargoniums too are available in an immense colour range right through the red-pink spectrum. If you grow your own bulbs, try peach or pink hyacinths and for summer some lilies suitable for pot cultivation.

An aechmea in full flower has stunning sugar pink mixed with pale silvery green and many of the bromeliads have quite strong red or pink colouration on their leaves. Bougainvillea and the Christmas cactus have brilliant magenta-pink flowers which are difficult to place. Few people use this brash colour in their interiors and these plants look best in plain white surroundings or in a conservatory where they can be toned down with plenty of fresh green. Both Dutch and oriental orchids are worth considering.

Pinks and mauvy greys harmonize beautifully to produce a bedroom with a lovely relaxing atmosphere. This colour scheme provides an attractive setting for foliage plants as well as flowering ones with blooms in the red-pink spectrum.

Blue can be a very difficult colour to use successfully but this quite daring mix of cool blues and warmer mauves works very well. The plants and flowers, particularly the hydrangeas, are the vital link between the hues. The containers have been carefully chosen to harmonize with the surroundings.

Mauves and Blues

Pure blue flowers are not among the most common. Many flowers calling themselves blue are more often than not mauve or at least blue with a hint of pink in their makeup. Blues of different kinds seem at first not to mix happily but as long as they have a liberal dose of green with them, the greeny blues and mauvy blues can be used together. Blue is considered too cool a colour to use often in the home, though at one time nearly every bathroom was painted a chilly 'aqua' or 'seaspray', only emphasizing the freezing conditions found in most bathrooms then. Blue looks at its best where it is mixed with plenty of white rather as on old china plates where the contrast makes the dark blue look fresh and clean. Large areas of flat blue paint or wallpaper can add space to a cramped room and certainly pale blue plus green remind us strongly of outdoors – green grass and summer skies stretching into infinity. The key to blue, though, is to add some green life to it to avoid the chill or blankness it can so easily spread across a room. Greyish blues are easier to work with and grey can always be warmed by a hint of pink, not green or yellow as they produce a hospital-corridor effect.

There are many blue-flowering house-plants which presumably shows our love of the colour. A few are true blue, some verge towards mauve and purple, and there are a few foliage plants such as *Sedum sieboldii*

which have a steely glaucous colour which looks good in blue interiors. The pretty trailing *Campanula isophylla* comes in a pale-blue version and makes a splendid hanging pot or basket plant though its effect is subtle. Hydrangeas come in blue and make a strong impression. They are particularly effective placed low on a table in a shallow container. *Plumbago capensis* is smothered in the palest blue flowers during late summer and autumn but is really a plant for a cool greenhouse or conservatory rather than in-doors. Stronger blues and purples are well provided for by such plants as African violets, cinerarias, streptocarpus and ex-acum, and during winter and spring a bowl of blue hyacinths gives a wonderful lift to any room. For a softer effect try the multi-flora hyacinths which have several stems of flowers with none of the stiffness of the usual type, and have a magnificent scent. Morning glories have the bluest of blue flowers and are well worth growing to stand in a sunny window for the summer. If you want your blues more subtle, try a foliage plant such as *Eucalyptus globulus*, which has marvellous blue-green leaves as do some sedum species and other succulents. In the vast cacti family there are many types with grey or bluish colouring. The bromeliad *Tillandsia cyanea* would make an interesting choice. The bracts have violet-blue flowers which can measure 5cm (2in) across. An arrangement of several different types looks marvellous.

A sunny yellow room feels summery even in the middle of winter. A large shallow basketful of chrysanthemums perfectly matches the yellow cotton upholstery, and the spider plants add a lush garden feel. The importance of being lavish with plants clearly shows here. One flowering plant would have looked bitty and mean, whereas this has real impact.

Yellows and creams

Yellow means warmth and sunshine, light and brightness. Golden yellow is not commonly used on large areas in interiors but toned down with white or cream the softer shades of sand and butter yellow are very popular. As in nature large patches of bright yellow need the contrast of plenty of green to cool them down. Imagine a bed of daffodils in strong sunlight then imagine the same flowers planted in grass. The first is overpowering, the second is calmer and much more pleasing. Yellow and green is one of the freshest combinations you can use. To make it sparkle even more add lots of white too. Creamy-yellow rooms need a highlight or two of brighter yellow and there are plenty of flowering houseplants which come in all shades of yellow from pale primrose to chrysanthemum gold to fill the bill. The hybrid broom *Cytisus×racemosa* has brilliant yellow flowers which smother the plant, almost obscuring the foliage beneath. It flowers from winter to early summer and likes plenty of light. It is a little tempermental and requires special attention. Many spring flowers, especially bulbs, are yellow – daffodils and crocus, tulips and pale lemon hyacinths. A favourite colour for chrysanthemums is rich golden yellow, and there are softer creamier colour variations too. Some orchids can be found in shades of yellow and the calceolarias have plain and spotted yellow varieties. A few foliage plants have golden versions or simply leaves which are splashed or edged with cream or yellow. Crotons often have wonderful yellow and red markings and the aphelandra has bold cream veining on its leaves plus a brilliant yellow cockscomb flower. The little primroses, grown as houseplants from Christmas onwards through to spring, are available in ever brighter colours year after year but somehow the original yellow type retains the freshness of the wild flower and by some strange trick always appears to have more scent than the other ones. A basket of four or five pots of yellow primroses is a marvellous cheer up for a kitchen or dining room table on long dreary winter days.

Chrysanthemums and primroses add the finishing touch to this brilliant white and yellow kitchen. This scheme would work equally well for both modern and traditional rooms.

This pale green and cream room takes most of its colour from the plants in it. They are the dominant feature. Everything else, especially the soft furnishings, is very understated and subtle. The tall tree is a Ficus benjamina. There is a small tolmeia under the lamp.

Greens

Green is a popular colour for many rooms. It is calm and restful and provides a good background for other colours that might be used with it. It has always looked good with wood and therefore with traditional furniture. Green reminds us of the countryside and natural things and gives us a feeling of space and quiet even in a busy city setting. It comes in dozens of variations and, as in nature, mixing greens together is usually very successful. There are not only bright acid greens and strong emeralds but also pale almond greens and the subtle colours of moss. Most of the dark or intense greens

need plenty of white used with them to work well, but the paler shades are successful when used in large areas with perhaps some darker green plus one or two colour accents.

Most colour schemes benefit from the addition of a different colour, not necessarily a contrasting one, to emphasize the quality of the main colour. Green seems to need this extra touch more than any other colour so that a small amount of pink or yellow or blue can lift a green scheme enormously and bring it alive in a quite spectacular way. In a garden we may miss the subtlety of the green foliage until we see it in relation to a colourful flower. There are plenty of gardens

created from just foliage but this takes great skill to make enough interest simply by shape and the subtle variations of green leaves and their textures. Indoors, because of the furnishings, this problem does not exist quite to the same degree.

A totally green room filled with plenty of plants creates an impression of outdoors inside; wonderfully cool in the summer, it can feel chilly in the winter. Bright, strong greens are best used sparingly in kitchens, bathrooms or children's rooms, while all the pale soft greens can be used successfully in living rooms, halls and bedrooms. They all benefit from plenty of foliage plants; flower-ing plants also look good against a back-ground of green. If you plan to have a room with lots of different foliage plants then consider how many shades of green there are available. Some such as the fern *Asple-nium nidus* have bright lime-green glossy leaves as does the maidenhair fern, while plants in the spathiphyllum family, for exam-ple, tend to have very dark-green leaves. In between the two extremes are dozens of shades and textures. Some plants have soft downy leaves, such as the African violet; others in complete contrast, such as the aechmeas from the bromeliad family, have sharp spiny-edged, leathery leaves.

The contrast between the light green fern and the darker ficus in the corner of the room gives a second tonal dimension to this green and beige room. The blue table and lamp shade provide a striking colour highlight.

Silver and variegated foliage

Once you have discovered the hundreds of different variations on a green theme there are, it is worth exploring still further towards the more subtle colouring found in the silver- and grey-leaved plants and those which are variegated. Variegation is the feature present when a plant has areas of its leaves with colours other than the green of the rest of the plant. What may have happened as an aberration in a plant is spotted by the plant breeder and developed and used to best advantage. Some people don't like their plants variegated, others can't get enough and collect masses of examples for their gardens or greenhouses. There are many houseplants now which have variegated plain green versions and there are some plants which are only ever seen in their variegated forms.

Silver- and grey-leaved plants are commonly grown outdoors to provide relief and contrast amongst brighter greens and it seems sensible to use this trick indoors too, adding one or two to a collection of foliage plants. Some plants in the begonia family have remarkable silvery leaves with a real metallic sheen to them. *Begonia metallica* and forms of B. *rex* are two to look out for. They are worth growing simply for their marvel-

The caladium is one of the most stunning variegated plants. It looks almost unreal with its delicate green tracery on a papery white background. It can be a little difficult to place and needs other plants around it. This group includes Pellaea rotundifolia, a dracaena and a startling caladium.

A group of eye-catching caladiums is the main feature of this collection of variegated plants, which also includes mother-of-thousands and a begonia. The group is the sole provider of colour in this all-white room.

lous leaves. *Zebrina pendula* has silvery leaves with a splash of green down the centre and is wonderfully easy to grow. Similar in leaf shape is the well-known tradescantia which is often overlooked but has the most beautiful cream-striped leaves. Many of the small-leaved ivies, bred especially for indoors, are variegated with either cream-edged or blotched leaves. Others appear to be splashed or spotted with silver or cream.

New varieties keep appearing with new colour variations. The scindapsus family which is similar to the philodendrons has many versions with silver, cream or golden markings. The pretty little plant *Plectranthus*

coleoides 'Marginatus' has beautiful creamy-white edgings and splashes on every wavy leaf. In the peperomia family there are several exciting variegated types. Of the larger foliage plants look out for variegated forms of ficus, fatsia and fatshedera. There are many silver- or grey-leaved plants. One of the most spectacular is *Rechsteineria leucotricha*, which has soft silky leaves like velvet. The plant with the most silver-coloured foliage of any is the cactus *Cephalocereus senilis* whose long white hairs fully covering the plant are reminiscent of a silvery beard and are responsible for the common name, old man cactus.

Multicoloured plants

This sitting room has a very busy mixture of pattern and colour, although all in pale soft colours. The plants and flowers used to complement the scheme are as varied in style and colour as the fabrics and accessories. The whole thing adds up to a very pretty, relaxed room.

Many people choose to decorate and furnish rooms quite simply these days. Plain carpets and small-scale patterned flooring designs are selling far better than they ever used to. Walls are often perfectly plain or with just the merest hint of texture or colour-on-colour. This all has probably a lot to do with the size of house that most people live in today. New houses are often scaled down to the minimum and, without a doubt, the simpler and plainer the interior is, the more a feeling of space will be created. It may be just that fashion dictates pale colours and

gentle fabric designs at the moment and before long there will be a great explosion of colour, and large bold designs will be in fashion again. But while we pass through a fairly restrained period in the history of home furnishings what we do need are flowers and plants to produce the spots of colour and the highlights to lift a simple scheme.

An all-white interior is the perfect setting for a few patches of brilliant colour and the stronger and bolder they are the better. In this situation you can mix colours together quite happily, sure in the knowledge that they can't fight with any others in the room. In a pale-grey room a mix of deep red and shocking pink plus green would work well and in a neutral room, with either cream or beige walls and floors, you could happily mix flowering plants with deep yellow, blue and red flowers. Brilliant red or deep rust looks marvellous with sand and caramel colours and bright sunshine yellow really lifts an all blue-and-white scheme. One successful mixture of plants which always seems to work is a collection of brightly coloured primroses. These can be found in purple, orange, bright pink, red and yellow. It seems unlikely that they could all work together without clashing. Somehow they do, probably because each plant has a good measure of green leaves to relieve the potent colours. In cases such as this choose a plant with good strength of colour and a fair amount of flower. A small-flowered plant from the other side of a room will make little or no impact but something such as an azalea or one of the flowering begonias really gives value for money in terms of the colour it provides. Hydrangeas too have plenty of petal power and so do lilies and many of the spring flowering bulbs.

A bold use of colour has really paid off in this fresh living room. Sensibly the walls and sofas were kept plain white and only a tiny amount of pattern used. Flowering plants in just one of the accent colours does not over clutter the effect.

Flower patterns

Flowers are the theme and inspiration for the fabrics, the screen and some of the ceramic pieces in this room. The choice of flowering plants is really very simple compared with the exotic blooms elsewhere in the room. The simple shapes and pretty colours work beautifully in contrast with the sophisticated furnishings.

Fabric designs over the centuries have mostly derived their inspiration from nature and in particular from plants and flowers. It is no different today: the largest choice in wallpapers and fabrics is still in the floral ranges. Even the occasional abstract design is more often than not based on natural forms. We all love flowers and therefore use them as decoration wherever possible. The choice is immense now and there is every style of design available from very smart, small-scale, all-over flower patterns to great splashy chintzes smothered with full-blown summer garden flowers, ideal for curtains.

Whatever you choose think how you might be able to link your choice with the plants you grow in your home. You can emphasize a fabric or wallpaper or perhaps a design on china with a clever juxtapositioning of the right flowering plant. A tiny spriggy flower print covering a bedroom could be echoed with a simple flowering plant which matches both colour and flower shape – a busy lizzie perhaps or an achimenes which both have rather flat, stylized flowers. A traditional chintz may have roses or peonies in its design which could obviously not be copied

indoors but a few fat mop-headed hydrangeas would introduce similar shapes in three dimensions. Lilies are another common theme and so are chrysanthemums, both flowers which can be grown indoors. If you enjoy visual puns try copying the contents of a flower print or picture in real life: a print of daffodils or pelargoniums, maybe with their real counterparts standing in front of them. There is no need to be quite so exact though and a flowering plant could be used simply to echo colours from a fabric. You will find that this has a way of highlighting a particular colour very strongly and you may even see the fabric or wallpaper in a totally different and unexpected way.

For a special table setting use a flowered cloth and pick out a colour and shape from it to carry through into a plant or group of plants. In summer, fresh flowers are obviously abundant but in winter, low flowering houseplants are very useful for table settings. Finally, do take another look at fabric or furnishings you may have lived with for years and see if, with a clever use of plants, you can freshen the whole room and maybe get some more mileage from what has been around for a long time.

Below Traditional leaf and flower patterns conjure up a beautiful cottagey feel to an interior They are best accompanied by simple foliage plants to prevent an over-fussy effect.

To contrast wittily with the curvy shapes on the walls a spiky architectural plant has been stood against the palm leaf greenery of the wallpaper. A brave choice which would work well in a hall or entance.

Leaf patterns

Leaf shapes crop up in fabric and wall-covering designs just as often as flowers. We may not always notice them as they often form part of the background but there are many designs based entirely on leaf forms in their own right. Some of the prettiest and freshest wallpapers are nothing more than a tracery of twining tiny leaves in green on white. There are also the beautiful William Morris designs, still produced after many decades and relying on flowing lines of many kinds of leaves to create an elegant and timeless pattern. In many of these designs it

is the shapes and quality of line which give them their style rather than colour, which is obviously so very important in a floral fabric or paper. With that in mind it is exciting and rewarding to use plants of all kinds to emphasize or harmonize with the designs in your house which are inspired by leaves.

A small-scale leaf-print wallpaper would look good used with a plant such as jasmine which has masses of tiny leaves and twining stems. Other plants with very small leaves include the asparagus fern and some of the pellonia family. Many lace designs which were so popular in Victorian and Edwardian

periods were based on leaf forms, particularly ferns, which were common both indoors and in outdoor fern gardens. Echo the fern leaves on a lace curtain with a real fern standing in front of the window. A tall plant stand containing a large specimen of a *Nephrolepis exaltata* would make a stunning focal point to a room. Some fabrics may contain actual leaf shapes which are recognizable, for example ivy, which you can easily pick out and highlight with real plants. Even designs which are rather vague and abstract may still contain shapes which can be identified as coming originally from particular types of plant – spiky iris leaves maybe, or the complicated cut-out shapes of a monstera.

Palms have dramatic and powerful forms and have inspired many designs, and the trailing twining habit of ivies and the hoya for example are suitable plants to reinforce the curving climbing shapes in some leafy fabrics and papers. Leaves alone are occasionally used as decoration on china, though it is far more common to see flowers as the influence. Sometimes leaves are used as a border or even in relief on plates or jugs and also on bowls.

A sensitive and clever use of leaf shapes suggests seaweed or underwater foliage in this tiny bathroom. The humble Sansevieria trifasciata 'Laurentii' *makes a stunning addition to these exotic conditions.*

Contrasts

The contrasts created in an interior are the highlights which give a room sparkle and interest. A simple plain all-one-colour room scheme looks restful and smart but a contrast provided by either colour, texture or style will lift it from becoming boring and highlight the points of interest. You can achieve contrasts in many different ways either by using permanent features such as furniture or fabrics or temporary things such as cushions, flowers or plants. With plants you may be as bold or safe as you like with your contrasts in the knowledge that if your ideas don't work you can always move the plants to a new position and try another effect. Colour has immediate impact and is probably the simplest way to make contrasts. Imagine a pale-green living room with a darker green carpet and curtains. If the furniture is of light coloured wood, the whole effect will be fairly bland but safe. Now add a bowl of brilliant pink cyclamen or a rich rusty-red amaryllis. The result is instant. The pink improves the greens and the soft background throws the flowers into relief. In the same way, bright yellows would bring a blue-and-white scheme alive and so

Right A cool hard-edged effect made by strong shapes and diagonals is cleverly contrasted by foliage in this blue and white kitchen and dining room.

Below Brilliant shocking-pink geraniums in a sky-blue pot give contrast in this plain white dining room, taking their cue from the tableware.

would mauvy blues and purples added to pale or sandy yellow.

The other way to produce contrasts is with forms and textures: straight lines with curves and fat round shapes with thin spiky ones. An example of this might be in a room with a crisp geometric trellis wallpaper. Here a plant with curvy leaf shapes such as a philodendron or caladium would make a perfect foil. In contrast, imagine a complicated swirling design on a wall with a stiff vertical plant such as a mother-in-law's tongue or billbergia standing in front of it. Contrasting textures is even more subtle and you may often achieve it without realising as when you place a velvety-leaved African violet on a smooth hard glossy piece of furniture. Plants by their very nature create contrasts in any room, which is bound to be made up of straight lines, hard edges and dead materials. A plant is living, even moving, and cannot help but produce a visual and physical contrast.

Asplenium nidus
Bird's nest fern
Height: 45-60cm (1½-2ft)
Spread: 30-45cm (1-1½ft)
Minimum winter temperature:
13°C (55°F).
An unusual fern, with large, wide, elongated spatula-shaped, bright-green leaves that form a shuttle-cock arrangement at their bases. These leaves differ from the normal deeply indented fern fronds in that they have entire edges.

Asplenium nidus

A peaty but open compost is needed, keeping it well-watered during summer but only just moist in winter. Clean the leaves regularly to remove dust and to enhance their appearance.

Begonia metallica
Height: 60-75cm (2-2½ft)
Spread: 45-60cm (1½-2ft)
Minimum winter temperature:
10°C (50°F).
Fibrous-rooted foliage begonia with a much branched framework bearing lustrous metal-green leaves with purplish veins. It is grown mainly for its leaves, but does also display pinkish-white flowers in September as a bonus.
John Innes potting compost

Begonia metallica

suits it. It prefers slight shade. Keep the compost moist during summer, and re-pot in spring if overcrowded.

Bougainvillea glabra
Height: 1.5-1.8m (5-6ft),
climber
Minimum winter temperature:
10°C (50°F).
A shrubby climbing plant. It is vigorous when in a greenhouse border but containable to the height given above when grown in 15-20cm (6-8in) pots. From late summer to autumn it displays the well-known clusters of small white flowers, 15-20cm (6-8in) wide, surrounded by rich red, purple-and-orange-shaded bracts. John Innes potting compost suits it well. Position in good light. Also ensure the plants do not dry out when in flower.

Campanula isophylla
Trailing bellflower
Italian bellflower
Star of Italy
Height: 10-15cm (4-6in)
Spread: 38-45cm (15-18in)
Minimum winter temperature:
2°C (36°F).
A beautiful trailing and flowering perennial, hardy outside only in the South and South-west, elsewhere best grown in a hanging-basket or

in a pot raised so that the stems bearing the dainty mid-green heart-shaped leaves and blue star-shaped flowers can trail during late summer and autumn.
For even more interest the variegated-leaved form *Campanula isophylla* 'Mayii' is worth considering, and for white flowers, *Campanula isophylla* 'Alba'.
After flowering cut off the trailing stems and keep the plant cool during winter, watering the compost sparingly. When new shoots appear in spring, slowly increase the amount of water and give a weak liquid feed.

Catharanthus roseus
often sold as
Vinca rosea
Height: 30-38cm (12-15in)
Spread: 38-45cm (15-18in)
Minimum winter temperature:
13°C (55°F).
A tropical periwinkle in the form of a tender, erect, evergreen, slightly shrubby plant. It displays glossy dark-green and rather longish oval leaves, with 2.5-4cm (1-1½in) wide rose-pink flowers from April to October.

Catharanthus roseus

Plants are available about late spring, and as long as the minimum temperature is maintained during winter the plants remain evergreen.

Cephalocereus senilis
Old man cactus
Height: 15-25cm (6-10in)
Spread: 5-7.5cm (2-3in)
Minimum winter temperature:
7°C (45°F).

Cephalocereus senilis

Distinctive cactus forming a round pillar, densely covered with long, whitish, silky hairs, looking very much like an old man's beard.
A well-drained compost is essential. Take care not to over-water it during winter. It prefers a bright sunny position.

Cineraria cruenta
Height: 38-45cm (15-18in)
Spread: 25-38cm (10-15in)
Minimum winter temperature:
8°C (46°F).
A beautiful December-to-June flowering houseplant, grown indoors as a biennial and best discarded after flowering. Its brightly coloured daisy-like flat or domed heads of flowers appear above mid-green, toothed-edged leaves. Flower colours include white, lavender, blue, pink and red. There are many in bi-coloured and double-flowered forms. John Innes potting compost is suitable. Make sure the plants are well watered when in flower as they quickly wilt. Raising the temperature by a few degrees encourages more rapid development of flowers.

Codiaeum variegatum pictum

Codiaeum variegatum pictum
Croton
Joseph's coat
Height: 45-60cm (1½-2ft)
Spread: 30-45cm (12-18in)
Minimum temperature: 16°C
(61°F).
Beautiful foliage houseplant
with a wide range of leaf
shape, from thin and ribbon-
like to spoon shaped and
branched. All have highly
coloured leaves in shades of
red, salmon and yellow. Many
named forms are available.
John Innes potting compost
suits it well, and a position in
good light enhances the leaf
colours.

Eucalyptus globulus

Eucalyptus globulus
Height: 60cm-1.2m (2-4ft)
Spread: 30-45cm (1-1½ft)
Minimum winter temperature:
2°C (36°F).
A beautiful, tender Gum tree.
In its native Tasmania it can
reach 15m (50ft). Its glaucous,
circular, stem-clinging greyish-
blue-green leaves, if crushed,
give off the well-known
eucalyptus oil aroma. The
adult leaves – often appearing
after two or three years – are
mid-green, large, long and
lance-shaped, but the plants
are not usually kept as long as
this.
John Innes potting compost
suits it, but as it grows rapidly
do not give it too large a pot.

Hydrangea macrophylla
Height: 38-45cm (15-18in)
Spread: 30-38cm (12-15in)
Minimum winter temperature:
7°C (45°F).
Easily identifiable flowering
houseplant with large,
globular flower heads, often
15-20cm (6-8in) wide and
packed with large florets.
Named forms are available in
cream, white, pink and blue.
Some have been artificially
induced to produce good
blues by ensuring the compost
is kept acid and by adding
aluminium sulphate.

Nephrolepis exaltata
Ladder fern
Height: 45-60cm (1½-2ft)
Spread: 90cm-1.2m (3-4ft)
Minimum winter temperature:
10°C (50°F).
A distinguished, delicate fern
for a hanging-basket or a plant
pedestal, displaying long,
finely crested, bright, fresh-
green fronds, often 60cm (2ft)
long and arching out from the
plant's base.
Many forms are available,
including the Boston fern
(Nephrolepis exaltata
'Bostoniensis') with wider
fronds; the Lace fern
(Nephrolepis exaltata
'Whitmannii') with finely
divided and graceful fronds,

Nephrolepis exaltata

ideal for a hanging-basket; and
Nephrolepis exaltata 'Todeoides'
with pale green and finely
divided feathery fronds.
These plants require a
compost formed of fibrous
peat, loam and sand – with the
addition of water-retentive
sphagnum moss, if set in a
hanging-basket.

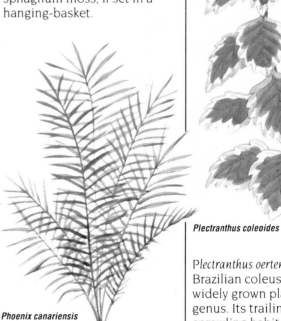

Phoenix canariensis

Phoenix canariensis
Date palm
Height: 1.5-1.8m (5-6ft)
Spread: 1.2-1.5m (4-5ft)
Minimum winter temperature:
10°C (50°F).
A beautiful palm with slender,
mid-green fronds rising from a
dense crown. The fronds arch

outwards and downwards.
John Innes potting compost
suits it well. Give it a lightly
shaded place in summer. Re-
pot in spring – usually
necessary only every two or
three years.

Plectranthus coleoides
Candle plant
Height: 30cm (1ft)
Spread: 25-30cm (10-12in)
Minimum winter temperature:
7°C (45°F).
A bushy, foliage houseplant
with roundish, hairy dark-
green leaves with scolloped
edges. The best form is
Plectrantus coleoides 'Marginatus'
having mid-green leaves with
clear white to light-green
edges, often with a greyish
sheen.

Plectranthus coleoides

Plectranthus oertendahlii, the
Brazilian coleus, is the most
widely grown plant in this
genus. Its trailing and
sprawling habit makes it
superb for a hanging-basket. It
has almost circular 5cm (2in)
wide bronze-green leaves with
silvery zones along the main
veins. The stems are reddish.
John Innes potting compost
suits it well. Re-pot and divide
overcrowded plants in spring.
Do not let the plants become
dry, especially during summer.

Primula sinensis

Primula sinensis
Chinese primula
Height: 20-25cm (8-10in)
Spread: 15-20cm (6-8in)
Minimum winter temperature:
10°C (50°F).

Enchanting perennial, grown as an annual to flower in the home from December to March. It produces thick stems bearing two or three whorls of flowers. The variety 'Dazzler' displays brilliant orange-scarlet flowers.
Give the same treatment as for *Primula malacoides* (see page 111).

Rechsteineria leucotricha

Rechsteineria leucotricha
Height: 23-38cm (9-15in)
Spread: 23-30cm (9-12in)
Minimum winter temperature:
16°C (61°F).

A tender tuberous-rooted herbaceous houseplant with saintpaulia-shaped roundish-oval, silvery-grey leaves covered with fine white hairs.

From August to October it displays 5cm (2in) long coral-red clusters of flowers from the upper leaf-joints.
John Innes potting compost or a peat-based type suits it well. Start the tubers into growth in a temperature of 21°C (70°F). Because of the high temperature initially required they are best bought when coming into flower.

Saintpaulia ionantha
African violet
Height: 7.5-10cm (3-4in)
Spread: 15-23cm (6-9in)
Minimum winter temperature:
13°C (55°F).

Popular houseplant having flowers most of the year but especially from June to late September. It displays oval, deep-green velvety leaves with heart-shaped bases. The round-petalled, single, purple flowers are borne in dense clustered heads above them. There are many varieties in a range of single, semi-double and double forms, from pure white though pink, carmine, red, mauve and purple to blue. Lime-free compost is necessary. Keep moist but not continually saturated, and position out of draughts.

Schlumbergera × buckleyi
Christmas cactus
Height: 15cm (6in)
Spread: 23-25cm (9-10in)
Minimum winter temperature:
13°C (55°F).

Schlumbergera buckleyi

Unusual Christmas succulent plant with flattened mid-green stems formed of indented, rounded sections, up to 4cm (1½in) long. From December to February it bears narrow trumpet-shaped magenta flowers, 5-7.5cm (2-3in) long. Well-drained compost is essential, but ensure that it does not dry out when the plant is in bud or they will fall. It is a suitable plant for a pot or hanging-basket.
This plant is often confused with the Easter cactus, *Rhipsalidopis gaertneri*, also sold as *Schlumbergera gaertneri*. This plant bears 6.5cm (2½in) wide bright red flowers during March and April.

Scindapsus aureus

Scindapsus aureus
Devil's ivy
Height: 1.2-1.8m (4-6ft),
climber
Minimum winter temperature:
10°C (50°F).

An interesting climbing foliage houseplant, often sold under its earlier name *Rhaphidophora aurea*, and occasionally under its new botanical name *Epipremnum aureum*. It is a useful houseplant, with broadly spear-shaped, bright-green leaves, flecked with yellow. As the plant matures the leaves become heart-shaped, and can grow to 30cm

(1ft) long. Several superb forms are available, such as *Scindapsus aureus* 'Marble Queen', with leaves dappled creamy-white.
John Innes potting compost or a peat-based type is suitable. Give slight shade during summer and ensure it is adequately watered.

Spathiphyllum wallisii

Spathiphyllum wallisii
Peace lily
Height: 23-30cm (9-12in)
Spread: 38-50cm (15-20in)
Minimum winter temperature:
10°C (50°F).

A beautifully foliaged flowering houseplant for centrally heated homes. It has bright, shiny green, spear-shaped leaves on long stems that splay outwards. From May to August it displays white, broad arum-lily-like spathes on long stems that peep above the leaves.
The hybrid *Spathiphyllum* × 'Mauna Loa' has larger spathes.
John Innes potting compost or a peat-based type is suitable, but keep it moist during summer. It is a plant that likes an even temperature, and a position away from draughts. A good light position in winter also suits it.

SEASONAL SPLENDOUR

Such numbers of houseplants are available these days all year round that we tend to forget there are many which are really only at their best at a particular season and in some cases have a distinct seasonal association, such as spring bulbs or the Christmas cactus. Others, such as the chrysanthemum, which used to be thought of as an autumn plant, can be induced to flower all year round by artificially manipulating the periods of light and dark. One can tire of these year-round plants and it is fun instead to reflect the seasons with what you have growing in your home. Here are some suggestions for different times of the year.

Flowering plants all have their moment of splendour when they reach their peak of colour and form. Here a wintery view is transformed by bowlfuls of cyclamen.

Spring sunshine warming brilliant pots of bulbs in a cottage window. Crocus, hyacinths, amaryllis and narcissi all vie for attention. The homely mixture of pretty bowls and containers really shows off bulbs at their best. Often the stems and leaves are tall and need disguising at their base.

Easter

From late winter through to early spring and Easter the house needs more than ever the cheerfulness and colour that plants can bring. The gradually lengthening days bring with them a flush of flowering plants and if you've planned ahead in the autumn you could have bulbs of all sizes blooming away for weeks on end. Easter wouldn't be quite right without daffodils and narcissi, and varieties such as 'Paper White' and 'Tete-a-Tete' are particularly suitable for pot culture. Primroses are real spring flowers, although we can buy them in pots right through the winter these days. Their bright jewel colours and wonderful fresh scent are welcome in any room. Surprisingly they are very effective when all the brilliant colours are mixed, perhaps six or so small pots grouped together in a shiny brass or copper container. For a more subtle arrangement use one colour at a time; there is nothing to beat the true pale primrose yellow. Other flowers in

bloom at Easter are cineraria in all shades of red, blue and purple, mimosa and jasmine and primula species such as P. *malacoides* and P. *obconica*. Most people know the Christmas cactus but there is also an Easter cactus flowering during spring with clusters of orangy-red flowers.

Many foliage plants which have been fairly dormant during the winter will be starting now to come back into active growth and will demand plenty of care and attention and possibly potting on into new pots or at least a change of compost ready for the summer. To show off spring flowers at their best it is most effective to have a great mass of plants together creating an outdoor flower border atmosphere inside. Many of the flowers at this time of year, notably crocuses and tulips, are quite simple with strong colours and look wonderful given this treatment. Fill in odd gaps with tiny pots of ferns or ivy or the very useful helxine with its solid mats of fresh green leaves.

Nothing cheers as much as crocus in full bloom. This group of white and yellow crocus have been planted with a small-leaved ivy to soften their outline. The turquoise basket looks just right. Try spray painting a plain basket to achieve this look.

Early summer

The growing season gets really underway in early summer when more and more plants appear. There are still bulbs which flower now such as tulips and sparaxis. It is probably best to cultivate these outdoors or in a cold greenhouse and simply bring them inside when they are about to flower.

Several species of abutilon are commonly available these days. They are graceful pretty plants with lobed leaves and hanging bell-shaped flowers, usually yellow or orange. Many annual plants make lovely, if short-lived, houseplants. Try growing schizanthus, the butterfly flower, which has stems simply smothered with flowers which come in an almost infinite colour range. Some forms are

rather tall, so choose one of the dwarf types and group several pots close together to make a really splendid show of colour. Pinching out the tips of the young plants makes for a good bushy shape. They won't need much warmth but plenty of light is necessary.

The hydrangea is another plant which seems to be available many months of the year and at this time there are some very good plants to buy and the colour choice is wide. One of the prettiest forms has a white flower with a hint of green and palest blue at its edges. If you can keep streptocarpus plants successfully from one year to the next they often start to bloom in early summer and carry on for several weeks and some-

Many annual garden flowers such as Lavatera trimestris do surprisingly well in pots. Lilium regale is one of the easiest lilies for pot culture. It is best to grow both these things outdoors and bring them in for flowering.

Gloxinias come in the most sumptuous range of rich glowing colours. Here more than one variety have been grouped in a basket for maximum effect on a dark wood dining table. They are rather formal and luxurious looking plants and look best with simple furnishings.

times for months. They are rather fussy about conditions and must have a cool and airy position with no direct sunlight which can scorch their thick brittle leaves, and must not be allowed to dry out. The colour range is through pink and blue to deep purple plus some white cultivars. Gloxinias are extremely showy plants. They are often sold at the point of flowering during the early summer months. Their large velvety leaves and trumpet-shaped flowers, often with frilly or crinkled edges, are very glamorous. However, they seem to be less popular than they were once. The choice of flower colour is enormous, ranging from white through purple to red and scarlet. Many varieties have bordered or spotted petals too. They are happiest in a slightly shady position with plenty of moisture when they are growing. A very pretty summery plant which seems to be perfectly designed for hanging pots or baskets is *Campanula isophylla*. It comes in both a pale-blue and a white-flowered version. The white version has slightly silvery leaves, which look good with the blooms. It is very similar to the small rock-garden types of campanula grown outdoors and has a delicate summery feel about it. After they have flowered, campanulas can be cut back hard in the autumn and kept slightly dry until the following spring when they can be brought back into growth.

Even if you have a garden to grow herbs in, it is fun and convenient to have some to hand in the kitchen. A surprising number do well in pots and many make pretty plants in their own right.

Late summer

Late summer in the garden is the time when plants settle down and flower happily for several weeks. Work done earlier in the year really pays off and it's time to sit back and enjoy the colour. It's rather easy to forget houseplants when so much time can be spent outside if the weather is fine. But there are many plants which are also at their best now and for many people in flats or without gardens the only summer garden they will have is an indoor one. The level of daylight is high which suits most houseplants, but don't forget they are also very prone to drying out during long hot spells and need careful watering. There are also the problems to be faced in going away on holiday and trying to keep plants healthy while you are out of the house.

Annuals sown in pots earlier in the year can make a superb display through the summer. *Thunbergia alata*, black-eyed Susan, is a good pot plant. It climbs or hangs, according to how you support it, although naturally it is a climber, and freely produces brilliant orange flowers with dark velvety eyes. Two or three plants grown to a pot make the best effect and they seem to suit a kitchen position or a cottage window as they are simple and quite unsophisticated.

Another annual that makes a lovely show is morning glory, which often fails outside if sown too early and then subjected to a cool summer. The most popular variety is still the sky-blue version though there are many different coloured forms on the market. They can grow up to 1.5m (5ft) given good conditions so allow for this by planting in a roomy pot and grow two or three plants to a pot. Provide canes and tie in the rapidly growing stems. A pot kept in a light and sunny place should give days and days of pleasure as each morning new flowers open.

Achimenes is a small-leaved plant which has a mass of little flowers rather like a streptocarpus blossom in shape. They are not as delicate or difficult as was once imagined and flower happily for several weeks throughout the summer. They are often pink but there are now many varieties in mauve, blue and white. Some types have a slightly trailing habit and make perfect hanging basket plants. They all like bright airy conditions. Pelargoniums may be more suited to life in a greenhouse or in tubs outside during summer months but it is fun to have one or two types on a window-sill indoors. They are simple, cheerful and very easy going. The scented leaf types are lovely to keep in a kitchen where the leaves can be pinched and the scent appreciated often. There are culinary forms whose leaves can be used in summer meals. Regal pelargoniums are often quite showy and grand, and, as their main flowering period is during late summer, make a perfect specimen plant for an important place in the house at this time of year.

Late summer is the perfect time for fuchsias and pelargoniums of all kinds. Fuchsias have a pretty, delicate look and there are dozens of varietes to choose from all in the pink, red, purple, white range. They like cool, moist conditions, not strong sunlight.

Autumn means warm glowing colours like those shown by this group of little purplish-pink ericas and red trumpeted fuchsia 'Thalia'. The Chinese lanterns have been picked ready for drying for the winter and make an attractive foil for the houseplants.

Autumn

As the days get shorter and colder we tend to turn back indoors to assess the pot plants in the house and generally tidy them up or perhaps move them to winter quarters. There are many plants which are at their best at this time of year and they are well worth finding and growing as it can be a difficult season for fresh flowers and many foliage plants are past their prime. The plant we most associated with autumn at one time was the chrysanthemum but of course these days it is available in flower all the year round. Dwarfed and controlled, it has lost a lot of its character and to many people it simply looks wrong flowering in the spring or summer. During the autumn it seems right and the colours echo those of other autumn plants and the leaf colours outside.

A plant which is grown mainly for its spectacular cream striped foliage is *Aphelandra squarrosa* 'Louisae'. In late summer and autumn it produces strange yellow flowers at the tops of the stems which last for several weeks. Coming from Brazil it is surprising that this plant can survive quite low temperatures during the winter. Even so it prefers conditions not to drop below 10°C (50°F). A plant usually sold in summer and autumn is *Exacum affine*. It has small glossy leaves and

pretty pale mauve flowers with yellow centres. This plant flowers for several weeks and is then discarded, but while it flourishes it makes a perfect houseplant. It is quite easy to raise from seed. Sow about four or five to a pot and pinch out the tips of the tiny seedlings to help them develop into sturdy bushy plants. A real autumn beauty is the colchicum or autumn crocus. Corms can be bought in late summer and planted in deep pots or simply stood on a saucer in a window-sill. The flowers appear on their own and the leaves come later in the spring. When the corm has finished flowering put the whole thing in the garden to continue growing. A highly exotic choice of plant, which flowers from summer through the autumn, is *Stephanotis floribunda*. It is a climber and is usually sold trained over a hoop. There is nothing to stop you from training it as you want it or for a particular position. It has thick glossy evergreen leaves and white waxy star-shaped flowers which have the most delicious scent. They like a slightly shady position with humidity and should be freely watered when in active growth. A mature plant could grow to about 3m (10ft) in height if you succeed with it so provide a suitable pot and scope for it to climb if it wants to.

Christmas

At Christmas time most houses are smothered in decorations, which tend to overshadow any plants they might already have. Luckily there are some highly dramatic and seasonal plants which can stand up well to the glitter and tinsel competition. An enormous number of plants as well as bowl arrangements and special things such as bottle gardens are given as presents at Christmas. It is easy in the excitement and flurry of the season to neglect plants so keep an eye on them all, especially any new ones, and perhaps give them a while to acclimatise to your conditions as they may have come from somewhere with quite a different environment.

The number one plant at Christmas must surely be the poinsettia which has become almost traditional now, presumably because of its red and green colouring. These plants are specially treated to delay their development until December and dwarfed to keep them compact, so it isn't sensible to treat them as a perennial but just enjoy them while they are at their best and keep them fairly humid and, if possible, at an even temperature. There are different coloured versions available but the red one remains the Christmas favourite. Another plant often forced for the Christmas period is the little erica, or heather, often seen in florist shops. There are two types widely grown, a white- or pink-flowered type and a pink with white-tipped flowers. They are neat and pretty and very cheerful winter plants.

A plant named after this time of year is the Christmas cactus (*Schlumbergera × buckleyi*). A well-grown plant in full bloom can be a spectacular sight in midwinter. The brilliant cerise flowers appear at the tips of the flattened leaf segments and the whole plant cascades downwards so it needs ideally to be stood on a plant stand or perhaps in a hanging basket. The flower formation is dependent on shortening day length so care has to be taken not to leave plants in autumn in lighted rooms during the evenings. Bearing this in mind Christmas flowering can be achieved year after year. The sweetly scented white-flowered jasmine is often bought as a present and will last well over the Christmas period and during the winter months. Yet another Christmas gift is a pot of hyacinths. They are always a pleasure even for their scent alone and well worth planting for yourself in case you are not given some. The bulbs must be planted in August/September; only specially prepared and forced bulbs will flower for Christmas so do check you have the right kind. An odd number of bulbs always looks

Poinsettias and candles together say Christmas. The deep-red foliage and the glowing candle flames complement each other beautifully. The little parcel candle holders provide the finishing touch.

best in a bowl, either three or five, and cover the bulb fibre on the surface with some moss as this makes the most enormous difference to the look of the thing. Often hyacinths are grown in bowls without drainage using special bulb fibre. It is fun to use all kinds of china containers such as old jelly moulds or unused vegetable dishes from a dinner service. An imaginative container adds a lot to an arrangement and looks far better than a thin plastic bowl.

Winter

During the long winter months we are most in need of a reminder that spring will come eventually and the dark gloomy weeks won't go on for ever, however much we feel they will on a raw wet December or February day. It is paricularly when Christmas and New Year are over and before the lengthening days have brought an improvement in the weather that we really appreciate the range of houseplants available at this season. Many are flowering and add colour, interest and scent to the whole house.

A very popular winter plant is the cyclamen bred from the delicate tiny *Cyclamen persicum* found in the Eastern Mediterranean area. Over the years larger and larger flowers have been produced and unfortunately the scent has mostly vanished. There are, however, some smaller more dainty types grown which retain their beautiful scent. Many people find cyclamen difficult, possibly because they give them conditions which are too hot or overwater them to the point of rot. They prefer cool conditions but not fluctuating temperatures or strong sun. This way they can be kept from year to year.

Another winter flowerer is the azalea, which usually comes in two main types: the Indian azalea which is tender, and the hardy Japanese type, most commonly seen growing outdoors. The tender one can be spectacular with its large, often semi-double, blossoms which can be red, pink or white. The hardy types also come in pretty coral shades, which are useful colours in many houses. Azaleas must be kept moist when in full growth and after flowering, in the summer months, plunged outdoors for the plant to recover and the wood to ripen for the

following year. Some people manage to keep plants growing for year after year when the azalea will grown into a small shrubby bush.

A plant totally different in style to the elegant azalea is the columnea. It needs to be grown in a hanging basket as its long trails of leaves can reach 90cm (nearly 3ft). There are various types, some with yellow flowers, others with scarlet or orange flowers. They are often grown under glass but will be happy as houseplants as long as the atmosphere around them is not too dry. One final winter plant which is bright and jolly rather than beautiful is the capsicum. These are ornamental peppers and according to variety bear little red fruits which are not poisonous like those of the solanums. They are easy to look after but are not perennial.

Winter can offer a marvellous range of flowering plants to cheer the long days. Indian azaleas are among the most attractive. They must be kept moist and not too hot. With luck and a little skill they can be kept for another year.

Abutilon × hybridum
Height: 60cm-1m (2-3½ft)
Spread: 45-60cm (1½-2ft)
Minimum winter temperature:
13°C (55°F).
Delightful pot plant with three-
to five-lobed, palm-like mid-
green leaves and pendant
funnel-shaped yellow, red and
orange flowers, 4cm (1½in)
long, from spring to autumn.
Several named varieties are
available, including the well-
known 'Ashford Red' with
salmon-red flowers and

Abutilon hybridum

'Golden Fleece' with rich
yellow flowers.
A shaded position is needed
during the height of summer
to ensure that the compost
does not become dry.

Aphelandra squarrosa
Zebra plant
Height: 25-45cm (10-18in)
Spread: 25-30cm (10-12in)
Minimum winter temperature:
10°C (50°F).
This is one of the most striking
evergreen foliage and
flowering houseplants. It has
large, spear-shaped dark-green
leaves, up to 23cm (9in) long,
with the veins lined in ivory.
From July to September it
produces four-sided cone-
shaped flower spikes in bright

Aphelandra squarrosa

yellow. The form *Aphelandra
squarrosa* 'Louisae' is superb,
with white veins.
John Innes potting compost
suits it well. Re-pot root-
packed pots in spring. Ensure
the compost does not become
dry during summer when the
plant is in flower.

Capsicum annuum
Red pepper
Green pepper
Chilli
Height: 30-45cm (1-1½ft)
Spread: 38-45cm (15-18in)
Minimum winter temperature:
7°C (45°F).
An attractive, neat, bushy plant
for the home, famed for its

Capsicum annuum

bright red berries, often
present as early as August and
lasting into the New Year.
There are many varieties
available, in a range of heights
and with variously shaped and
coloured berries – green,
violet, yellow, red and rose-
coloured, and in shapes from
oblong to globular.
The plants are usually bought
when displaying berries and
require a cool, light, airy
position away from draughts.
Avoid high and rapidly
fluctuating temperatures.

Columnea gloriosa
Gold fish plant
Trailing stems up to 1m (3½ft)
long
Minimum winter temperature:
13°C (55°F).

Columnea gloriosa

Delightful hanging-basket,
evergreen plant, with spear-
shaped, slightly fleshy, pale-
green hairy leaves borne in
pairs. From October to April it
displays hooded, bright-red
flowers with yellow markings
in their throats. The form
Columnea gloriosa 'Purpurea'
displays leaves tinted purple.
Similar plants include
Columnea microphylla which has
pendulous stems up to 1.5m
(5ft) long and many orange-
scarlet flowers from November
to April. The hybrid *Columnea*

× *banksii* bears reddish-orange
flowers with orange throat
markings.
Peat-based composts suit
them. Keep it moist during the
flowering period.

Erica gracilis

Erica gracilis
Height: 30-45cm (1-1½ft)
Spread: 20-30cm (8-12in)
Minimum winter temperature:
5°C (41°F).
A popular winter-flowering
heather frequently grown as a
houseplant. It has pale-green
leaves and terminal, somewhat
pyramidal heads of globe-
shaped, rose-purple flowers
from October to January.
Erica hiemalis is also used in
homes and has November-to-
January tubular white flowers
with a pink flush.
An acid compost is essential.
At no time should the plants
experience high temperatures.

Exacum affine
Arabian violet
Persian violet
Height: 23-30cm (9-12in)
Spread: 20-25cm (8-10in)
Minimum temperature: 13°C
(55°F).
A pretty, delicately flowered
annual houseplant with oval,
mid- to deep-green shiny
leaves and purple, saucer-
shaped, violet-like mauve
flowers with yellow centres
from July to September. The
variety 'Starlight Fragrance' is

Exacum affine

superb, having a delightful fragrance.
It is best bought when just coming into bloom and given a position free from draughts and strong sunlight. Keep the plants well watered and discard them after flowering.

Fittonia verschaffeltii 'Argyroneura' Snakeskin plant Lace leaf

Height: 7.5-10cm (3-4in), trailing
Minimum winter temperature: 16°C (61°F).
Eye-catching trailing foliage houseplant with oval to spear-shaped 7.5-10cm (3-4in) long leaves, dark green and with the veins lined in ivory-white.
Fittonia verschaffeltii displays slightly larger leaves, and the veining is not so delicate and fine. However, it does not require such a high temperature, 13°C (55°F).

Fittonia verschaffeltii

John Innes potting compost or a peat-based type suits it well. Keep the compost moist during summer. The plant benefits from high humidity.

Narcissus – Garden forms Daffodils

Height: 30-45cm (12-18in)
Spread: 7.5-10cm (3-4in)
Minimum winter temperature: 7°C (45°F).
These garden harbingers of spring are also suitable for indoors, and will flower from Christmas to early spring. They can be bought in pots ready for flowering indoors; alternatively, specially prepared bulbs are available in early autumn which should be potted up firmly, watered and placed in a cool vermin-proof position for twelve to fifteen weeks until the shoots are about 10cm (4in) long. Bring indoors and slowly raise the temperature from 7°C (45°F) to 15°C (60°F). Once the buds are showing colour reduce the temperature.

Primula malacoides

Primula malacoides Fairy primrose

Height: 30-38cm (12-15in)
Spread: 25-30cm (10-12in)
Minimum winter temperature: 10°C (50°F).
A delightful flowering houseplant, with December-to-April whorls of dainty, star-like flowers which can range from pale lilac-purple to white. Many named forms are available, some of a dwarf nature.

John Innes potting compost suits it well. Ensure that the compost is kept moist as the plant tends to wilt badly if kept dry.

Primula obconica

Height: 23-38cm (9-15in)
Spread: 25-30cm (10-12in)
Minimum winter temperature: 10°C (50°F).

Primula obconica

Well-known December-to-May flowering houseplant, with clusters of red, pink, lilac or blue-purple flowers with wavy edges. There are many varieties, some giant flowered with blooms up to 5cm (2in) wide.
Give the same treatment as for *Primula malacoides* (see above).

Schizanthus pinnatus

Schizanthus pinnatus Butterfly flower Poor man's orchid

Height: 25cm-1.2m (10in-4ft)
Spread: 25-60cm (10-24in)
Minimum temperature: 5°C (41°F).
Beautiful bushy annual plant for the home, with deeply divided fern-like, pale-green leaves smothered from spring to autumn with single, butterfly-like flowers up to 4cm (1½in) wide.
The colours include yellow, purple and rose, often with spots. Many varieties are available, from dwarf to giant types.
Plants are usually bought in flower and should be put in a light and airy place and kept well watered. Discard after flowering.

Thunbergia alata

Thunbergia alata Black-eyed Susan

Height: 1-1.5m (3½-5ft), climber
Minimum temperature: 10°C (50°F).
Well-known annual climber with mid-green ovate leaves. The five-petalled, orange-yellow flowers have chocolate-brown centres and are borne from June to September.
John Innes potting compost suits it. Provide a fan of bamboo canes or a trellis of plastic netting for it to climb up.

PLANT SETTINGS

An attractive setting or container is an important element in displaying houseplants. A fine plant can be twice as effective if stood in a handsome container or, in the case of plant arrangements, if the group is displayed in a well-chosen trough or on an attractive piece of furniture. When it comes to terraria and bottle gardens the choice of containers is perhaps easier as most vessels sold for these purposes are highly decorative, but more attention must be given here to what sort of container would look best in a particular situation – a faceted case in a period setting perhaps or a bottle garden in a more modern-style room. Whatever your preference in house-plant arrangements you will find that time taken thinking about containers will pay off.

The right choice of container is often as important as the houseplant itself. Here a group of quite different plants is held together by the use of basketwork containers.

One splendidly decorated cache-pot and stand dominates a beautifully balanced arrangement of plants. Sensibly, baskets instead of ceramic containers have been used for the other plants to let the cache-pot stand out.

Containers

As far as the plant is concerned, the container is perhaps not the most important factor, although the size does limit its growth. To us the container, or cachepot, is very important if we are thinking of plants as part of an overall scheme for a room, and nowadays there is no excuse for being unimaginative for there seems to be an ever increasing range of things to put our plants in. There is nothing more infuriating than to discover the attractive cachepot you have just bought does not fit the plant pot, so when buying one go armed with measurements or you may have to put up with an ugly plant pot edge sticking up above the rim of your new cachepot.

The first requirement of a plant is a good pot to hold the compost it is growing in. Certainly plastic pots are convenient for

azalea or a bright pelargonium, but rough terracotta may not look right on say a modern glossy piece of furniture or in a smoothly elegant bedroom. Clay pots were originally used with soil-based composts. They allowed moisture to evaporate through the sides, keeping the compost cool, but they had the disadvantage of drying out rapidly. There are some cases where plants are planted straight into a container such as a self-watering trough, but more often than not you need to start with some kind of small pot.

A row of plants lined up along a window-sill could be treated in several ways. If you have a good collection of clay pots all similar and standing in saucers, the plants grown in them will produce a good simple and straightforward effect. A motley collection of pots needs covering with either small baskets; a mix of different cachepots, say all white but in different shapes and sizes, or simply a row of blue-striped pudding basins. In a more formal setting there are dozens of plain or decorated china containers to choose from. Either tone in with colours already used in the furnishings or walls or choose bright contrasting colours or all-over patterns in a simple room scheme. Flowering plants look best in plain pots while duller foliage plants benefit enormously from a beautifully decorated container. Most cachepots without any kind of drainage should be safe standing straight onto furniture but check first on a place where a damp-ring doesn't matter: even some glazed pots have a nasty habit of ruining polished furniture. If in doubt stand them on saucers. Saucers are vital for most plants growing in their own pots as they help when watering and protect surfaces underneath them. There are now some lovely glazed pots often sold in twos or threes which come with ready-made saucers, or with one long one on which all the pots can sit along a shelf or window-sill.

The Victorians and Edwardians used spectacular great pots to stand their plants in. Many were stood on tall columns to show off perfectly a prized specimen of a palm, fern or aspidistra and they were placed in drawing rooms and halls as well as conservatories

growers as they are easy to clean and light to handle and can be easily transported from place to place. Plastic works well with the newer peat-based soilless composts and the rise of both has gone hand in hand. They are convenient for us too but they just don't look good. A plastic pot in nearly every case needs hiding. Clay pots, especially old ones, have a quality all of their own which is perfect for some plants such as an ancient

One pot alone might not be noticed but rows of them just can't be missed. This wicker shelf unit becomes an important feature with the help of these pretty matching flower-pots. The plants almost don't matter but African violets are just right.

which were immensely popular. Antique jardinieres can still be bought and there are plenty of reproduction versions as well.

Basketware seems to have a natural affinity for plants and there are many different types to choose from. Some baskets are specifically made to hold plants and many of them are lined with plastic. If you use one that is unprepared then stand a plant saucer in it or line it with plastic yourself. Groups of

large plants grouped on the ground look particularly casual and pretty arranged in wide shallow baskets. They appear lighter visually than they would do in a great solid ceramic or plastic container.

One way of displaying plants, which has become extremely popular, is to hang them in baskets or special containers. There are plenty of hanging plastic pots with built-in drip trays but they are less than beautiful indoors. Macramé hangers in which you put your own pot and saucer or a simple basket with handles either side are much nicer. They should be hung by strong cord to a hook or bracket on the wall or ceiling. For a more dramatic effect try spraying a wicker basket with cellulose paint as sold for cars. They are available in a wide range of colours and produce a bright durable result. A large plant plus soil and moisture can weigh a surprising amount so fix it securely to the wall or ceiling.

When thinking about containers for all your houseplants don't feel you have to use what is offered. It is well worth searching for any old and unusual things which will show off a plant well. It really doesn't matter what it was originally meant for, it is how it performs in its new rôle which is most important. An example of this might be a simple, brightly coloured, plastic wastepaper bin used for a tall foliage plant or an old lidless teapot used for a pretty African violet. Both of them will look just right.

An old or specially interesting container should hold simple plants, perhaps some healthy, glossy-leaved foliage ones such as here. Philodendron scandens and rhoicissus combine elegantly to show off the metal pot to its best advantage.

Terraria and glass cases

During the latter half of the 19th century, plant collectors sent back specimens to this country, housed in elaborate glass cases. The plants needed to be kept growing to survive their long journey, which might take months by boat and horse transport. In the 1890s a Dr. Nathaniel Ward discovered that small plants seemed to thrive when grown in an enclosed glass case where there was no moisture loss; any water transpiring from the plants found its way back to the soil via the glass roof and sides. In Victorian times, a real passion developed for growing plants indoors and in conservatories, and many complicated and quite beautiful miniature greenhouses were made to house collections of small plants. Today there is a revival of interest in this method of growing things and there are some pretty reproduction Wardian cases available, often sold ready planted by nurseries and garden centres. To achieve the same effect but with less expense it is possible to use any suitable glass container such as a fish tank. Plastics are not suitable for this. Moisture does not readily run off the surface and clouds it, preventing the plants from being seen. Also, plastics tend to crack in sunlight making the container unsightly and eventually useless.

Small-faceted cases look very attractive in their own right, especially amongst period furnishings, and even a simple tank-shaped case can usually be incorporated somewhere in a room. Whatever type of container you choose be sure that any water droplets

A very pretty and delicate glass case makes the perfect home for a white-flowered begonia. The flowers appear to float in the space, and sensibly only one other small-leaved plant has been used with it.

condensing on the roof will run down the sides of the case and not drip straight onto the plants. Most of the ready-made ones are designed to avoid this problem, but a fish tank will need the roof tipped at a slight angle to let the water run away. When you plant a terrarium, of whatever type, it is important to plan the position of the plants in relation to one another as you would in an outdoor garden. The container has to be seen in isolation and planned like a miniature border as it is more likely that it will be looked at as a feature in its own right and not as part of the room's decorative scheme.

Plants have to be chosen carefully for these rather special conditions and obvious-

ly the first consideration will be the size of container you are working with. Many small foliage plants thrive in the warm stable atmosphere provided by a terrarium, especially ones from the fern families and the dracaenas. Flowering plants tend to be larger and will need the height of a tall bell jar or similar container, but African violets seem to enjoy an enclosed environment and always stay neat and compact. In complete contrast to a moist lush indoor garden it is possible to use a ventilated glass container for a collection of cacti, arranging them to look as natural as possible. Several different forms planted together will give you an exciting result.

A large brandy goblet has been put to an original use here. Filled with water, it makes an attractive setting for a cryptanthus.

Bottle gardens

Growing a collection of plants in a large bottle or carboy is a variation on keeping them in a terrarium. A true bottle garden has a stoppered top and plants which are suitable can stay untouched for three years or even longer. The bottle must be clear or of pale-coloured glass and not dark brown which would not let enough light through. The top needs only to be wide enough to get the small plants through as planting is done with special tools and not with your hands. Usually a large carboy is planted standing upright and a container such as a tall, narrow sweet jar is used lying on its side.

The plants to choose for a bottle garden should be small and slow growing and be happy in moist shady positions. The compost should contain a small amount of crumbled charcoal to keep it fresh over the long period of time it will be in the jar. The special tools needed to plant things can be very simply made at home from small spoons, forks, wire loops and whatever, tied to thin bamboo canes. You will probably find that different devices suit different plants so experiment until you find what makes the

job easiest. A funnel with a piece of plastic tubing attached to the end is essential for pouring soil into the carboy and for watering. It will take a few days after planting for the atmosphere inside the jar to settle down; the glass will mist over at first and the

Above right The tools you need for bottle gardening are mostly everyday things. A little ingenuity is needed in making the long-handled fork and trowel.

Right The shape of container is up to you and the range of plants is enormous but keep to small-leaved varieties such as crassulas, Ficus pumila *and* fittonias.

A bottle garden does not have to be an enclosed moist environment but can be left open to grow small cacti which will thrive in draught-free conditions. A miniature landscape has been created from carefully selected cacti, planted in a layer of soil over sand.

lid should be left off until it clears. If the jar is stood in direct sun more moisture evaporates from the compost and the plants, and the glass mists over, so make sure the container has a permanent place in a sunless part of the room. Bottle gardens look good on a low table or shelf and very pretty effects can be achieved at night by positioning a light source just above them or behind them. Sometimes the glass jar is used as a base for a lamp but this can look rather strange and contrived and is not to be recommended. A better solution would be to have a bottle garden with a plain table lamp standing beside it.

The choice of plants for a bottle garden is really very wide once you understand their particular requirements. Tiny ferns of all types are ideal and mosses and some small bromeliads look perfect. Very small-leaved ivies are fine and so are fittonias. A few plants grow too well and start to crowd out the others so occasionally check the situation and prune or replant as necessary. You can add small pebbles and pieces of bark and other bits and pieces if you want to create a miniature landscape but don't overdo it as it is very easy to end up with a messy effect which detracts from the plants and upsets the overall impression.

Above A simple white unit is used for a display of foliage plants.
Right, top A stylish trough made from horizontal strips of bamboo perfectly sets off the vertical shapes of the aspidistras.
Right, bottom Beautifully curvy cream-coloured containers give a thirties feel to a group of tall plants on a plain, simple landing.

Troughs and large containers

A large plant or a group of them needs a container which is stable and has a big enough capacity for proper watering and maintenance. Many arrangements, especially the large-scale ones found in offices, restaurants and public buildings, are kept in troughs designed to need the minimum amount of care. Some have devices which regulate watering and have reservoirs that only need checking and topping up. Troughs meant for ordinary homes are more usually designed to hold several plants standing on a base of pebbles which can be watered easily, creating a humid atmosphere for the plants. The individual pots can be stood directly on the pebbles or grit, or damp peat can be packed round each to keep them even more moist and cool. A very big plant can be planted straight into a tub as one would do outdoors but here extra drainage must be provided. A tub large enough for this would be extremely heavy and care would be needed to position it safely, particularly on suspended floors.

Most troughs sold as indoor containers are usually made of plastic though it is possible to find timber ones. It is not too difficult to make simple wooden ones yourself. They can be painted or stained a good colour or simply sanded smooth and waxed or varnished. The simplest shapes such as a generously proportioned square or a long low rectangle, standing along a wall or beneath a window, usually look best. Very small blocks or balls of wood at each corner will keep the trough clear of the floor; taller legs look spindly and unsafe, and rather dated these days.

Choosing the best plants for display in a trough depends both on where it is to stand and the room conditions. A trough filled with individual plants in their own small pots can be changed frequently and varieties can be juggled to produce the best display at any one time. A more permanent arrangement needs to be planned carefully, with the plants put in according to height, leaf shape and colour. Remember to use plenty of small low-growing plants to cover ugly plant pots and gaps. A few tiny trailing foliage plants or a carpet of helxine amongst the larger plants would solve the problem and do much to improve the overall effect.

Display tables and arrangements

There is no doubt that a group of several small foliage and flowering plants arranged together in a large decorative container looks far more impressive in a room than the same plants dotted about here and there. Put together, one slightly insignificant plant is improved by a more flamboyant one, similarly a plain-leaved variety is thrown into contrast beside its variegated cousin.

The simplest way of achieving the maximum effect from a few small plants is to stand them within a bigger container, perhaps a basket or a china washbowl, and move them about to find the best positions. Small bowls are often planted with several different plants and sent as gifts. These can last for many months but if planted with rather incompatible plants, one type may grow faster than the others, or the plants may suffer and die due to inadequate drainage. If you make this kind of planting yourself you can make sure that a bowl without drainage holes has a layer of gravel at the base and a well aerated compost is used. On a slightly larger scale, groups of plants look good arranged on a table or similar surface still standing in individual pots. Keeping several plants together in this way cuts down on their moisture loss and gives a more natural appearance. Plants in the wild seldom stand isolated except perhaps for a few very large trees and most of those prefer the shelter of a forest.

It is fun to arrange a group of plants in one area, planning which way they should face and what should stand next to what. A table against a backdrop of some kind will need higher plants standing near the back, sloping down to low ones at the front. A mixture of leaf shapes is vitally important using some broad flat leaves and some thin strap-shaped ones, some with cut or serrated edges and perhaps a heart-shaped variety such as a *Philodendron scandens*. Too many similarly sized plants squashed close together can look fussy and confused. It is better by far to limit yourself to a few really good-looking specimens leaving plenty of space around them yet letting the shapes of the leaves break across each other. You can aim for symmetry or have a totally lop-sided arrangement, the position of the table in the room probably being a deciding factor.

Sometimes a plant display of just one variety will have a more stunning effect than a mixture where the impact of well-chosen superb plants has been diluted by inferior ones. A group of cyclamen all in flower, maybe in various shades of one colour, would look best standing alone. An arrangement of ferns using all the different types but not adding other kinds of foliage plants would make a very strong impression.

Houseplants are expensive items and it is worthwhile equipping yourself with a few proprietary chemicals so that you can combat the pests and diseases that indoor plants are prone to. Only chemicals specifically formulated for the purpose should be used on indoor plants. A list is given here of the more common problems you are likely to come across and how to treat and, where possible, to avoid them.

Pests

Greenfly (aphids). Plumpish green insects (with or without wings) that feed on the sap of soft-tissued plants, distorting their leaves and shoots. They often transmit virus diseases. They cluster on the undersides of leaves and around new shoots and buds, excreting a sticky honeydew that encourages sooty moulds, which mar the appearance of the plant.
Control: spray with pyrethrum and resmethrin, pirimicarb or permethrin.

Whitefly. Small white flies, rather triangular in shape. The young nymphs live on the undersides of leaves, sucking sap and excreting honeydew. When disturbed they dart about quickly.
Control: spray as for greenfly. Repeat at intervals of 10 days until irradicated.

Red spider mites. Tiny (almost invisible) brownish-red or straw-coloured 'spiders' that feed on the undersides of leaves. They suck sap causing mottling. Cobwebs may occur between the leaves.
Control: spray with pyrethrum and resmethrin.

Mealy bugs. The white, wax-covered adult females resemble small woodlice. All stages of this pest feed on the plant's sap. Leaf-joints and bases are usually the first parts attacked.
Control: spray with malathion or dimethoate (do this outside), then pick off the insects.

Scale insects. These troublesome and persistent pests often form dense colonies of static, waxy-brown or straw-coloured female insects. They lay eggs under their body scales, where they hatch, spreading the infestation.
Control: spray as for mealy bugs.

Diseases and Disorders

Greymould (botrytis). A widespread and troublesome disease of soft-tissued plants. It appears as a fluffy greyish mould on the leaves and young shoots. Saintpaulias, gloxinias, cyclamen and gynura plants are especially susceptible.
Control: remove all affected tissue and spray with benomyl or thiophanate-methyl (do this outside). Avoid cold, damp, still conditions, which encourage the disease.

Rust. Raised reddish-brown spots often surrounded by dead tissue. Chrysanthemums, cinerarias, pelargoniums and fuchsias are especially susceptible.
Control: there is no effective treatment. Destroy the plant to prevent it infecting others.

Powdery mildew. A powdery white coating on stems and leaves, and sometimes on the flowers.
Control: remove and burn infected parts. Spray with benomyl or thiophanate-methyl. Position plants in a well-ventilated place.

Greenfly.

Whitefly.

Red spider mite blotching.

Mealy bug.

Wilting. Plants may wilt as a result of too much or insufficient water, or being attacked at the roots by pests.

Insufficient moisture obviously results in wilting, and usually the plant recovers when given water. However, there is a wilting point from which the plant will not recover, irrespective of how much water is subsequently given. Occasionally a plant will wilt even though it has been given the right amount of water. If it is placed in strong direct sunlight, for instance, water will evaporate from the leaves more quickly than it can be taken up by the roots and the leaves will droop. However, this is nautral and the plant will recover in the evening.

Excessive watering and keeping the compost totally saturated will eventually kill the roots and the plant will die. If you suspect this is happening, stop watering. Where there is a good dense root ball to hold the compost together, a water-logged plant can be dried out by removing it from the pot and exposing the soil ball to the air until most of the water has evaporated.

Pests such as root aphids and root mealy bugs graze on the roots of pot plants, causing wilting. They can usually be seen if the plant is removed from its pot. They can be controlled by watering the compost with diazinon.

Bud drop. The dropping of buds and flowers. It may be caused by draughts, a dry atmosphere, sudden chill, too much or too little water.

Leaves yellow and fall. If the leaves drop rapidly, the plant has probably received a sudden shock, perhaps due to a rapid change in temperature. This often happens to plants bought during winter and exposed to extremely cold temperatures on the way home. If the leaves turn yellow slowly, not falling straight away, the cause is probably too much water. However, if the leaves turn yellow but do not drop the cause could be too much lime in the compost or water.

Hygiene and Safety

Every year children are rushed to hospital because they have come into contact with a garden chemical. Household pets can also be affected. Yet all of this can be prevented by following a few simple rules. Many modern plant chemicals are potent and highly toxic, and must be handled with care and used exactly as the manufacturer's recommendation.

- Read the instructions on the container before using – not during or after.
- Only use those chemicals in the home that are recommended for such use. Some are only suitable outdoors.
- Avoid bringing chemicals into contact with polished surfaces or fabrics.
- Do not allow sprays to come into contact with animals or fish.
- Never store chemicals indoors; they are best placed in a lockable cupboard in the garage or shed. Never pour them into other containers, such as lemonade bottles, that children might find appealing.
- If possible move the plants outdoors to be sprayed. If the weather is unsuitable spray in the garage or place the plant in an empty plastic dust-bin beforehand.
- Always use rubber gloves, and immediately wash off chemicals that have splashed on to your skin. If any splashes into your eyes, wash with water and consult a doctor immediately.

Scale insect.

Greymould.

Rust.

Wilting due to dryness.

INDEX

Page numbers in *italic* refer to illustrations and captions; those in **bold** refer to main plant descriptions

Acknowledgments

Special Photography:
John Bellars 24-5, 28-9, 60, 78-9, 82-3, 90-1.

The publishers thank the following individuals and organizations for providing the photographs in this book:

Michael Boys Syndication 18 above, 19, 28, 37, 38, 41, 54, 55, 66, 86, 88, 90, 101, 123; Linda Burgess 6-7, 100, 102, 106-7, 109, 112-3; Mike Burgess 64-5, 114-5; Camera Press (Avotakka) 18 below, (Femina) 2-3, 26, 69, 94 below, 122, (IMS) 14, 15, 16, 27, 40, 108, 119, (Koteliesi) 11, (Px/Sy) 94 above, (Schöner Wohnen) 50, 80-1, (SK) 59, 72, 87, 120 below, 121, (Zuhause) 8-9; Good Housekeeping (Jan Baldwin) 98-9, (David Brittain) 85, (John Cook) 71; Melvin Grey/Octopus Books 34-5, 39, 67, 68, 120 above; Susan Griggs Agency/Michael Boys 12, 22, 53, 105, 116; Robert Harding Picture Library 56; John Harris/Octopus Books 48; Holt Studios 125 left and right; Bill McLaughlin 51, John Moss/Octopus Books 117; Octopus Library 104, 124 right and far right, John Sims/Octopus 124 left and far left, 125 far left and far right; Jessica Strang 73, (Benjamin) 23, (Morrison) 70; Elizabeth Whiting and Associates 1, 10, 13, 17, 20, 21, 24, 36, 42, 43, 46, 49, 57, 58, 76-7, 78, 82, 84, 89, 92, 93, 103, 118.

Illustrations on pages 25, 29, 79, 83, 91, by Tony Hannaford. Plant illustrations by Tim Hayward and Stuart Lafford.